Marcus Dods

The post-exilian Prophets

Haggai, Zechariah, Malachi

Marcus Dods

The post-exilian Prophets
Haggai, Zechariah, Malachi

ISBN/EAN: 9783337067922

Printed in Europe, USA, Canada, Australia, Japan

Cover: Foto ©Lupo / pixelio.de

More available books at **www.hansebooks.com**

HANDBOOKS

FOR

BIBLE CLASSES.

EDITED BY

REV. MARCUS DODS, D.D.,

AND

REV. ALEXANDER WHYTE, M.A.

EDINBURGH:
T. & T. CLARK, 38 GEORGE STREET.
1879.

'Then the angel that talked with me answered and said unto me, thou not what these be? And I said, No, my lord.'

> 'Thou speakest mysteries; still methinks I know
> To disengage the tangle of thy words:
> Yet rather would I hear thy angel voice
> Than for myself be thy interpreter.'

THE
POST-EXILIAN PROPHETS

HAGGAI
ZECHARIAH
MALACHI

With Introductions and Notes

BY

MARCUS DODS, D.D.

EDINBURGH
T. & T. CLARK, 38 GEORGE STREET
1879

PRINTED BY MORRISON AND GIBB,

FOR

T. & T. CLARK, EDINBURGH.

LONDON, .	. HAMILTON, ADAMS, AND CO.
DUBLIN,	. ROBERTSON AND CO.
NEW YORK, .	. SCRIBNER AND WELFORD.

PREFATORY NOTE.

IT has long been felt by some of those whose business it is to teach "Bible classes,"—whether in the church, the school, or the family,—that their work might be greatly assisted could they direct their pupils to suitable text-books. But although in every other branch of education there is an abundance of manuals suitable for primary and secondary instruction, and prepared by men who are recognised authorities in their respective departments, the immense stores of Biblical learning which have now been accumulated have not been made accessible to the young scholar. The present enterprise—which was projected before any similar series was announced—is an attempt to provide trustworthy manuals of Biblical knowledge, some of which may be found better adapted for instruction in elementary schools, while others may be found more suitable for young men attending our universities and who are attracted by serious study. There is also reason to believe that such manuals will be welcomed by many private readers of Holy Scripture. The Editors consider themselves fortunate in securing the very hearty co-operation of men who are undoubtedly competent to carry out this idea.

M. D.
A. W.

GENERAL INTRODUCTION.

THE PROPHETS AND PROPHECY.

PARTLY from accidental circumstances and partly from their nature, the prophetic writings have not received from the ordinary Bible reader that share of attention which they deserve. There are many persons who have no taste for poetry, and who have a positive repugnance to poetry which is also obscure. They have therefore no patience with some of the profoundest and most elevating writing of our own and other times. They will not condescend to read a line twice over: they throw aside whatever they do not comprehend at a first reading. Books which have stirred the best thoughts and awakened the deepest feelings of other men, it is needless to invite such persons to read. Poetry such as Robert Browning's must be to them a sealed book. But the writings of the prophets belong to precisely this species of literature. They are poetry, and they are also obscure. They are poetry of the most unintelligible kind, full of rapid transitions, obscure allusions, highly imaginative representations. So that if the prosaic reader, who finds he can only here and there pick out a verse or two of which he can make what he calls "sense," should with some irritation demand why such a style has been adopted, it must in the first place be replied that this is a style into which many of the highest literary efforts in all ages have run and must run, and that if he cannot command patience slowly to find out the meaning, he must lose much of what is most important and stirring in the word of God, but for this loss must blame himself and not the prophets.

But many who are at some pains to understand the prophetic writings, are yet unable to conceal from themselves some disappointment and annoyance at finding them so often unintelligible. We feel the power of their highly-wrought visions of future peace and holiness; their enthusiasm and impassioned eloquence carry us away; the very rhythm and fall of the sentences fascinate us; ever and anon a clause of eternal significance sinks deep into the heart or pierces the conscience: yet passages continually occur which stumble us by their obscurity. Even in the most frequently-read passages, and in those which have always exerted a powerful influence on the mind and spirit, there occur sonorous sentences which move us as the tones of an organ do, but which convey to the mind quite as little intelligible meaning. Who has not been annoyed in reading, say, the twenty-fourth of Isaiah, to be thrown out by such clauses, and to have his devotional feeling changed into bewilderment?

Now, no doubt this obscurity is greater than it need be. In our present English version of the Bible, the prophetic writings are both imperfectly arranged and imperfectly translated. They are arranged not, as we should naturally expect, in chronological order, but apparently according to their length or supposed importance, if, indeed, any principle has been adhered to in the matter. Manifestly we are thus put at a great disadvantage for understanding the prophets. They were a series of men, not disconnected individuals. They were sent by God one after another to complete gradually the whole revelation He designed to make. They were usually sent in connection with events then happening; and to ignore all this arrangement, and treat them as if they might as well have spoken in any other order and at any other time than they did, is to lose a great deal both of the interest which attaches to the lives of the prophets, and of the point of their predictions. If a mass of correspondence is put into our hands, the first step we take towards understanding it is to arrange the letters according to their dates. All is confusion till we do so; till we know what years the letters were written in, and what domestic and public events were transpiring in those years, we cannot hope to understand the allusions made by the writers to these events. A thousand points of great significance, if taken in connection with certain days and events, lose all meaning if read out of that connection. But it is thus that we read the prophets, and then complain that they are uninteresting and unintelligible.

It is an immense help, then, to our understanding of the prophets, when we take the trouble to place them in their proper chronological order, and read them in the light of the events which called for their encouraging, warning, or fault-finding utterances. Besides, it is only thus that we can at all discern the growth of prophecy from age to age. The prophets were employed by God to carry out a plan which included the whole period from the beginning to the coming of Christ. Each new revelation adds something to that which had before been delivered. The prophets themselves, consciously or unconsciously, fell in with this plan. They were thoroughly conversant with one another's writings, and by the study of the existing prophetic literature they understood something of the lines on which prophecy travelled; so that we often find a later prophet quoting the words of an earlier, but never going back and speaking as if at a more rudimentary stage.

The dates at which some of the prophets exercised their function have been much disputed; but the following may be accepted as an approximate chronology:—

Prophet	Date	Period
Jonah,	840 B.C.	
Joel,	810	} Early part of Uzziah's reign.
Amos,	810	
Hosea,	810	} Uzziah, Jotham, Ahaz, and Hezekiah.
Micah,	765–699	
Isaiah,	759–699	
Nahum,	c. 636.	} Josiah.
Zephaniah,	641–609 or 611	
Habakkuk,	c. 610	
Jeremiah,	628–585	
Obadiah,	599	} Captivity.
Ezekiel,	595–574	
Daniel,	606–534	

POST-CAPTIVITY.

Haggai,	. . .	520.
Zechariah,	. . .	520–518 [490?].
Malachi,	. . .	425.

History of the Prophetic Order.—There is evidence in the O. T. that the prophets of Israel from a very early period formed a guild or fraternity. The first notice we find of such an association occurs during the life of Samuel. It would appear that in his day prophets existed in some considerable numbers, and that they were to be found occasionally, if not usually, in bands or companies (1 Sam. x. 5, 10, 11). A permanent settlement was formed for them at Naioth, that is, in the *meadows* or open pastures around Ramah, and over this settlement Samuel himself presided (1 Sam. xix. 18–24), and probably endeavoured not merely to instruct them in music, but to imbue them with his own religious zeal and energetic patriotism. The history of this particular brotherhood or "school of the prophets" it is impossible to trace; but that, even after the strong personal influence of Samuel was withdrawn, the numbers of the "sons of the prophets" were maintained, we gather from several allusions to them as a recognised and influential body in Israel. Two centuries after the time of Samuel, Obadiah was able to save 100 prophets from the rage of Jezebel (1 Kings xviii. 4); and even after the persecution by Jezebel, King Ahab had no difficulty in assembling 400 prophets when he wished to consult them on a matter of state (1 Kings xxii. 6). From the frequent allusions during the period of Elisha to the schools of the prophets, it is obvious that these had now become a national institution. They were not now confined to one locality, but are found at Bethel, at Gilgal, and at Jericho. And as these localities are only incidentally mentioned, it is possible similar associations existed at other convenient places. That they had received either from Elijah or Elisha, or both, a fresh impulse, is apparent from the deputation which waited on Elisha, representing that their accommodation was no longer adequate for their growing numbers. Further down in the history no allusions occur to the schools of the prophets; but as far down as the captivity "the prophets" are spoken of as an influential and probably numerous body of men (Jer. iv. 9, xxix. 1).

These scattered notices establish the fact that the prophets of Israel were a permanent order of men, and not a broken and incoherent series of individuals appearing one by one at long intervals. Behind the inspired men whose writings we possess, and who are therefore most important to us, there appears a body of men permanently recognised among the Hebrews as the prophetic order. They were marked out to the public eye by the usual distinguishing features of such fraternities. They lived together and took their meals together, the Gilgal school sitting down together to the number of one hundred men (2 Kings iv. 43). But unlike the modern fraternities with which we naturally associate such cœnobitic life, the members might marry (2 Kings iv. 1). Their dress was peculiar, so that as among ourselves certain orders of men, and even some of their religious distinctions, may be recognised on the street by the dress they wear, the prophets of Israel were recognisable by their garment of hair. Elijah is described as "an hairy man with a leathern girdle," which apparently means that he wore the usual dress of the prophet, the camel's hair cloak girt with leather. It is the same dress which was many centuries later assumed by the last of the O. T. prophets, John the Baptist—a dress which he chose not as a piece of "self-inflicted asceticism," but merely to claim kindred with the great order to which he belonged. It is this fact, that the garment of hair was the prophet's peculiar dress, which explains to us the words of Zechariah (xiii. 4): "In that day, the prophets shall be ashamed every one of his vision; neither shall they wear a *rough garment* to deceive"—that is to say, they shall not dare to assume the ordinary dress of the prophet which might induce people to listen to their words. And for the same reason, because the garment was peculiar, the one thing by which the prophet was recognisable to the eye, the mantle became the symbol of his power. Elisha assumed that which had been worn by Elijah as if virtue resided in it.

Employments of the Prophetic Order. — How this large body of men found employment, either while in residence with the fraternity to which they belonged, or when living with their own families, it is not easy to say. Only one thing appears certain, and that is, that they were considered to possess extraordinary insight, and were consulted regarding all doubtful matters, both public and private. If the king was in doubt whether war should be declared, he consulted the prophets. If a farm-servant lost his asses, after exhausting his own detective ingenuity, he repaired to the prophet, and for a small gratuity received the desired information as to the whereabouts of the missing beasts. These responses given by the prophets were accounted oracular and were accepted as the voice of God. "Beforetime in Israel, when a man went *to enquire of God*, thus he spake, Come and let us go to the seer: for he that is now called a Prophet [*nabi*] was beforetime called a Seer [*roeh*]" (1 Sam. ix. 9). Being thus accredited with superhuman insight, they were naturally resorted to for medical advice. The case of Isaiah, not only predicting Hezekiah's recovery but prescribing for him, may be considered scarcely a case in point; but the application of Naaman the Syrian leper to the prophet of Israel can hardly be a solitary or exceptional case. This is in keeping, too, with the common usage of the East (though not of Egypt), in which the hakim or sage is usually the physician. There is a stage in the development of heathen society in which the functions of seer, judge, physician, and priest, are all exercised by one man; and at the analogous stage in the development of Israel, the prophets seem to have been resorted to in cases of sickness where other skill had failed, in cases of casuistry too hard for the elders, in cases of law where the priest acknowledged that some new points had emerged involving new principles regarding which he could not certainly deduce from the law of Moses.

Abuse of their Position.—Obviously such a body of men could not long resist the deteriorating influences which naturally attached to their position. "Power shows what a man is;" much more does it test a corporate society. For many will attach themselves to it for the sake of the power. The gifts and bribes bestowed on the prophets must at times have been very large, although it is to the credit of the order that their wealth seems at no time to have been great, and certainly never in any way comparable to the enormous accumulations of the Delphian oracle. But a position in which private and public affairs can be controlled, a position in which one's own ideas will be accepted as authoritative, and one's own person venerated, offers of itself too strong a temptation for ordinary human nature to withstand. Accordingly, in this as in other similar societies, degeneration went rapidly on, until in the days of Jeremiah the prophets were the most hurtful element in the community, distinguished above others for the vices peculiar to their calling,—covetousness and falsehood,—and indeed sunk to the level of the heathen augur or the barbarian diviner who feigns a nearness to God that he does not feel, and works himself up into a paroxysm of unnatural excitement which the gaping multitude mistakes for inspiration. "A wonderful and horrible thing," says Jeremiah, "is committed in the land; the prophets prophesy falsely, and the priests bear rule by their means; and my people love to have it so: and what will ye do in the end thereof?"

Relation of the Prophetic Order to the Prophets whose Writings we possess.—Not all, then, who were trained in the schools of the prophets were true prophets: nor were all true prophets trained in these schools. Looking at the original institution under Samuel, we might have expected this prophetic order to be a flexible supplement to the standing institutions of Judaism. It seems to give promise of an institution which is not restricted by fixed law as the priesthood is, but which can expand and develope alongside of, and in correspondence with the growing wants and aspirations of the people; and which is not liable to the deleterious influence of hereditary exclusiveness, as both monarchy and priesthood were, but was open to receive at all times whoever was ardent in patriotism or felt a natural leaning to spiritual avocations. It seemed admirably adapted to a nation which was destined to live in a special communication with heaven. It was fitted to be the channel through which guidance in occasional emergencies and instructions for new developments could be received. But when the order became corrupt, and the prophetic body contained rather those who made pretensions to supernatural afflatus and insight than those who really lived near to God and were imbued with His wisdom, the "word of God" came not to one who was professionally and nominally a prophet, but to him who was already in spirit at one with God; and "the word" coming to such a man, it made him a prophet. The call of God was unrestricted: tied "to no institution nor to any class. It might come to an Amos, gaining a scanty living by his own labour; it might come to the young priest Jeremiah, dwelling on his own lands at the priests' town Anathoth; it might come to Zephaniah, a prince of the blood royal, amid the splendours of a court."[1]

Yet there seems some reason to believe that even those inspired prophets who held themselves aloof from the association of men popularly known in their day as the prophetic order, were yet indebted to this order in more respects than one. Manifestly for an easy introduction to their office, they were indebted to the circumstance that prophecy was already a recognised feature of Israelitish society. Besides this, the later prophets were probably indebted to the prophetic fraternity, the schools or sons of the prophets, for their knowledge of the utterances of previous prophets. Isaiah quotes from Micah, a contemporary of his own, in a manner which indicates that he was quoting either from a written book, or from carefully-guarded oral tradition. Obadiah quotes in the same way from Jeremiah. Amos takes up the very words of Joel and uses them as his own introduction, and for his conclusion he can find no fitter words than those of the same prophet. It has been observed that "the prophets use the same metaphors, dwell in the same circle of thoughts, employ the same phrases, have certain expressions always recurring in the same meaning,"[2] and from this it has been concluded with much plausibility that "they had some common centre, some headquarters where they met, and where the young were educated, and the inspired writings of the great prophets were made available for general use and study." It is natural to suppose that these centres were the schools of the prophets. And thus these establishments, though insufficient to produce by any training of theirs a body of inspired men, did serve the very useful purpose of

---

[1] Payne Smith's *Bampton Lectures*, p. 113.   [2] *Ibid.* p. 142.

maintaining the common prophetic tradition; of giving to the men who were to be used by God for revealing new truth, the suitable preparation of a knowledge of what had already been delivered, and also of preserving their utterances in turn either in an oral or a written form.

In addition to this, it has been supposed by some that the prophetic order disseminated among the people a knowledge of the revelations made to the inspired prophets—that they formed, in fact, a kind of clergy or ministry among the Jews. Certainly there was abundant room for such a body of teachers of the people. Until the Captivity there seems to have been among the Hebrews no regular instruction in religion apart from what a father might feel himself qualified and disposed to impart to his family. The ministry of God's word, which in the Christian Church is the great standing means of grace, was not a stated ordinance among the Jews. The Levites were, indeed, charged to study and teach the law; but this trust they seemed to themselves adequately to discharge by answering inquiries regarding obscure points of law, or difficult questions of casuistry. Prophecy itself was intermittent, and the words even of an Isaiah seem to have been but once uttered by himself, and could not reach the ears of the whole people unless by the intervention of intermediate teachers. And it has been supposed that this function was discharged by the ordinary members of the prophetic body; and that as our Lord's disciples treasured His words in their memories, and spent their lives in extending the knowledge of truth which had at first been delivered by Him to a dozen, or a score, or a hundred people, so did these earlier disciples of the great prophets diffuse the knowledge which otherwise must have been confined within very narrow limits. It cannot be said, however, that this has been established on sufficient evidence.[1]

How the Prophets delivered their Message.—The manner in which

---

[1] "The pastoral office, so far as it did then exist, was discharged by the prophets or those trained under their superintendence. For it seems to have been the custom for these inspired teachers to gather round themselves associations of disciples, or students, who lived together under a common rule, and who frequently appear in Scripture under the title of the sons of the prophets; from which notices it may

the O. T. prophets themselves delivered their message is strikingly different from the manner in which heathen prophets deliver their oracular responses. Here there is no sitting on a tripod, or entering a gas-charged cave, no whirling or dancing till convulsions and frothing at the lips supervene. The Hebrew prophets are found on the spot where their message is needed, in the temple courts, in the king's palace, on the public streets. The only aid they used to give effect to their teaching was symbolic action : a device which has its root in human nature, and is suitable in every age and nation. Tarquin lopped off the heads of the tallest poppies with his cane, to suggest a diabolical device he dared not put in words. The Scythians, when anxious to persuade Darius of the hopelessness of invading their territory, instead of making a long harangue, argued with much more force by bringing him a bird, a mouse, a frog, and two arrows, to signify that unless he could soar like a bird, burrow like a mouse, or hide in the marshes like a frog, he would never be able to escape their shafts. So, when Saul rent Samuel's garment (1 Sam. xv. 27), the prophet said, " The Lord hath rent the kingdom from thee this day." So did Ahijah the Shilonite not content himself with predicting that Jeroboam should have ten tribes as his kingdom, but rent his garment into twelve pieces and gave him ten of them. Ezekiel was especially partial to this mode of teaching. One day he might be seen sitting on the ground and portraying on a tile the siege of Jerusalem, or making little models of battering-rams and other engines of war, and moving them against the model city until its walls fell in ruins. Or, again, he might be seen pulling down the earthen wall of his own cottage, and carrying out his furniture and household articles in the twilight as one who was going into captivity; or, with a yet more fantastic symbolism, he lay for upwards of a year in one position, as if crushed to the earth by the burden of his people's iniquity ; or, with a still bolder and more pointed imagery, he might be seen setting on a pot filled with

likewise be gathered that they existed in considerable numbers. Instructed thus by one himself taught of God, they became fitted to teach others ; and we cannot doubt that by their means the knowledge of divine truth, in its various stages of communication, became widely disseminated amongst the people " (*Litton*, p. 156).

meat, pointing out to those of his fellow-captives who gathered round him how filthy a city Jerusalem had become, a city from which the scum had not been removed, but which had been boiled and boiled and boiled till all that was in it had become scum, and had caked itself in the pot and marred it utterly.

Mode of Prophetic Revelation.—If we inquire into the mode by which God revealed Himself and His truth to those who for Him were to publish it to all, we must set distinctly before our minds, in the first place, the fact that revelation is a spiritual process which we cannot detect and trace during its operation; and we must put aside our natural but erroneous idea, that an impression made through the senses is both more profound and more trustworthy, and especially more objective, than impressions made by spiritual means. For what we mean by *revelation* is that certain men come to have thoughts about God and divine things not only new in the world and more significant than other men have had, but also such as they themselves could not have conceived or arrived at without the extraordinary aid and suggestion of God Himself. Even when the thoughts may seem to grow up in their mind as other thoughts do, they are not their own thoughts, but God's. Though the revelation is made within the prophet's mind, and by a process which he may not always be able to distinguish from his ordinary habit of thinking, the matter conveyed to his mind is as truly a revelation from God as if it were uttered by a voice from heaven, or written with a supernatural finger. This is what is essential in revelation, that it be God's utterance to us—God not waiting for men to find Him out, but Himself coming and giving us sure knowledge of Himself. Eminently helpful are the reflections which careful observers of the ways of God may make on any occurrence; eminently enlightening and suggestive are the ideas which a mind experienced in human character may give us regarding the Divine; but revelation is not the sum of the happiest guesses or wisest observations and reflections which devout and thoughtful men have made regarding God, but it is the sum of what God Himself has imparted to the minds of men to guide and rule their thoughts about Him.

Sometimes, no doubt, supernatural communications were made to the prophets by means of visions and dreams. But even in dreams the mind is not wholly passive. A dream is commonly engendered in the mind out of materials prepared by the waking hours. And so in the waking vision, doubtless that man was chosen for the reception of the vision whose face was turned in its direction, and whose eye was educated to see it. The dream in which the fate of the world's greatest empires was disclosed was the dream of the man whose waking thoughts were all of empire, and the interpretation of it was imparted through the man whose mind had been prepared for such a knowledge by being exercised in matters of state. And even in the visions of Zechariah, it is obvious that what was thus revealed to him, his own mind was prepared to see and appreciate by its previous activity concerning the matters on which light was thrown. In the majority of the prophets there is no appearance of anything like absolute passivity, but rather there is evidence of the highest energy of both mental and spiritual faculties. There are undoubtedly instances in Scripture of persons being thrown into that ecstatic condition which resembles the state in which heathen priestesses delivered their responses, and in which certain oriental enthusiasts appear to be capable of superhuman feats. But of this state psychology can as yet give us only an imperfect apprehension, and it was certainly not in an ecstatic condition that the prophets of Scripture commonly exercised their function. With them there was nothing resembling possession; there was no loss of self-control, no excitement, no suspension of any faculty which ordinarily characterized the man.

On the contrary, we see that those to whom God's word came were the men who habitually were most concerned about the condition and prospects of His people. The convictions regarding conduct, which they were commissioned to produce in others, were first of all wrought in themselves. The word they declared was no word mechanically learned and easily uttered; it was a word which had grown up out of the convictions and views of things slowly wrought in them by their own divinely-guided experience. Like all other great teachers, they could teach best what they had first lived; they could teach not by book-learning nor by acute observation of other men,

but by that sympathy with them and understanding of them which
their own conflict had imparted. Into Ezekiel's hand there was put
a roll written within and without with lamentations and mournings
and woe, an objective revelation which he himself had not written;
but before he could deliver it to others, he had to eat it: all that was
written on it had to become a part of himself, had to be taken into
his inmost experience and be digested by him, and become his own
very life's blood. It is thus made plain to us, that in revelation the
operation of the Divine Spirit is for the most part conditioned by
the state of the recipient mind, and that no prophet could receive
and still less communicate knowledge which was not capable of
being assimilated to the previous contents of his own mind.

Authentication of the Prophet's Mission.—This being so, it may be
thought that men might sometimes mistake their own thoughts for
the thoughts of God; and there is no lack of instances recorded in
Scripture in which men either made or professed to make this fatal
confusion. The wonder is there are not more; but probably men
were deterred from wilful imposition by the capital penalty attached
by the law of Moses to false prophesying. Among the prophets
whose writings we possess, some were very sparing in their communications, and others seem to have prophesied almost against their
will. Their long intervals of silence, too, even after they had gained
a reputation, are particularly instructive in this connection. For
example, Zechariah had no visions for two years after the first dis-
closures; he had nothing which he could honestly communicate to
the people as fresh from God. To those who enjoyed his visions
and waited for them more impatiently than we wait for a great
speech from a leading statesman, or a new poem from the laureate,
this was no doubt disappointing; and strong pressure must have
been put upon him to produce some new deliverances. Matters were
all the while turning up which it was a strong temptation to decide
by some supposed oracle; questions were no doubt constantly put
to Zechariah, about which he had his own private opinion, which it
must have been a strong temptation to give out as authoritative.
But Zechariah was an honest man, and a man of clear inward vision,
who could not mistake his own imaginings and judgments for what

was distinctively God's word in him; so that the people would gradually come to see that prophecy was not of any private instigation, was not the imaginings of the individual prophet, but that the prophet was then only a prophet when he spoke as he was moved by the Holy Ghost.

Wherever, then, the test prescribed in Deut. xviii. could not be applied, we have the prophet's own consciousness taken in connection with his general character, and especially in connection with the message he declares, to authenticate his mission. There is never any doubt apparent in the prophet's own mind. He is clear that his words are from God. There is a burden laid upon him; he is called irresistibly to speak what God has given him to say. Such a consciousness in the mind of men uniformly on the right side, seeking neither gain, nor power, nor applause, but, on the contrary, often incurring reproach, and ill-usage, and sometimes death,—such a consciousness co-existing with views of public affairs which prove the prophets to be no fanatics, but men of sobriety and wisdom,—goes far to be its own best evidence.

Nature of Prophecy.—These remarks upon the soil out of which prophecy sprang, and upon some of the more obvious and outward characteristics of the prophets, may serve to familiarize the mind with the subject, and may prepare us to form a judgment of this remarkable mode of revelation. Prophecy is the necessary attendant of God's revelation of Himself in the history of Israel. God designed to make a personal manifestation of Himself in human history. Historical circumstances, place and time fit, must be prepared that this manifestation may be congruous, understood, and utilized. For this end He chose Israel, and by a long-continued process educated them to know Him, to wait for His salvation, to furnish Him with a sphere of life in which it was possible for Him to manifest His glory. The Jewish people existed for a special and declared object, and throughout their whole history, and in their entire constitution, this object was kept in view by the hand that moulded and guided them. They were the tree out of which was to spring that Branch on which God was to find satisfactory fruit. The tree, therefore, was throughout its growth a prophecy of the Branch. Every detail of their constitution, every movement of their history, had a reference to the end for which they existed, and in so far prophesied of that end. The relation of God and man, which was perfectly accomplished in Christ, was throughout established between God and His people, though it could only be expressed in much less adequate forms than the humanity of the Son of God. But all these forms, imperfect as they were, yet, being the work of God, were with promise, and carried in them the assurance of a perfect time still to come. The nation itself, therefore, and all the representative personages, critical events, and essential institutions, were prophetic. They all existed for the sake of the future which existed in the design of God. "A mild and lambent light of prophecy," says Frederic Myers, "may be considered as encircling their whole constitution and attending their whole history, which, though condensing itself at times into a brightness which the dimmest eye might discern, for the most part was rather a luminous atmosphere than an orbed blaze."

The relation which the spoken word of the inspired prophet bore to this prophetic people and history is obvious. The prophets were needed to guide the nation in its destined course towards that goal of blessing to mankind; they were needed to remind the people of their God, their Law, and their Covenant, to prevent them from competing with other nations and for worldly objects, to maintain their supernaturalism, and so be the very sap of the growing tree. Without these men it is impossible to see how faith and hope could have been maintained in Israel at all.

Kinds and Varieties of Prophecy.—Since prophecy is thus the handmaid of Jewish history, or the pilot of it, it will be Messianic in the same proportion as the history is Messianic. Accordingly it is commonly and justly said that *all* prophecy is Messianic. "The longing after deliverance, and after the full appearance of the divine salvation and the divine rest, pervades the whole history of the Israelites, . . and this longing more or less prevails in the predictions of all the prophets, and forms the horizon to which every glance is directed."[1] It will, however, be found to simplify

[1] Bleek's *Introduction to Old Testament*, ii. 30.

the interpretation of prophecy, if the reader attempts to classify the prophecies. One classification may be stated, although others may be found both more exhaustive and more helpful. According to their fulfilment, prophecies fall into two great classes—those which were fulfilled in the Messiah and His times, and those which were fulfilled previously to these times. The second class presents fewer difficulties, and may be dismissed in a sentence or two.

Prophecies fulfilled in the Time of the Prophet himself and before the Time of the Messiah.—To this class belongs, *e.g.*, the well-known prediction in Zech. iv. : " The hands of Zerubbabel have laid the foundation of this house ; his hands shall also finish it." This was a prophecy which bore its meaning on its face, and for its interpretation or fulfilment needed no reference to a distant future. Sometimes a prediction of this sort may be so wrapped up in figurative language as to be slightly disguised ; but, generally speaking, there is no difficulty in interpreting predictions which are intended for immediate fulfilment, if only the historical circumstances be well understood.

Prophecies fulfilled in the Times of the Messiah. — That the Jews did, for many centuries, look for a great king to arise in the line of David, who should establish a perfect kingdom of God upon earth, is beyond dispute. Differences of opinion might exist regarding the time of His coming, or the signs of it, or the nature of His person, or the characteristics of His kingdom, but no Jew doubted that the Messiah would come and reign upon earth. This singular expectation survived to the time of our Lord. There were at the time of His birth still some who "waited for the consolation of Israel." The scribes and lawyers had still their theories regarding the place of His birth, and the manner in which He was to be heralded to His throne. So universal was the hope, that even a degraded Samaritan woman could say that, as a matter of course, she knew "that Messias cometh."

From the original announcement of redemption recorded in the third chapter of Genesis, down to the accomplishment of redemption by our Lord, the Messianic idea was in process of formation. At first vague and general, it gradually became precise and well defined. In the first announcement there were disclosed two elements which were permanent—that the redemption was to be accomplished by a *person*, and that this person was to be human. It was the work of slowly evolving ages to develope this germ, and to elaborate a tolerably complete image of the person and work of the Redeemer. The first long and little-understood period of human history left as its result a broad distinction in character between three races of men ; and revelation, keeping step with history, then disclosed from which of these races the Redeemer was to spring. A shorter period sufficed to narrow down the expectation to a single nation. As time went on, a single tribe, and then a single family, was indicated as that from which the Redeemer was to arise.

This family was the reigning family in the still united kingdom— the family of David. From this time onwards, therefore, the Redeemer was marked out as a king. Without the slightest apparent vacillation of purpose during a thousand years, this line of David was unalterably regarded as that which should produce the Messiah. No other family or tribe was put in competition with the house of David in this matter. Even at the lowest ebb of the fortunes of that royal line, it was on it the eye of hope was turned. The function of prophecy henceforth was to quicken this hope, and to define with an always growing exactness the kind of kingdom which the Messiah was to establish. It would seem, indeed, as if in the youthful vigour of the kingdom, amidst all the fresh bursting life of the spring-time under David and Solomon, men had no provocation to look forward. The actual kingdom was enough to occupy their thoughts and satisfy their ambition. Such Messianic allusions as belong to this period are for the most part not purely Messianic, but are idealized representations of the then existing state of things. But with national disasters and disappointments, civil discord, a growing corruption in all ranks, and a black political outlook, there were generated a sense of the meagreness and transitoriness of the glory that was and had been, and a craving for the ideal kingdom, and a demand for prophets—for men who could tell them of the kingdom of God upon earth, and guide them towards it through present disaster and perplexity.

But the change which we describe in a sentence, it took two centuries to produce. For apparently the first result of the reign of Solomon was to deaden the minds of men, and only slowly and painfully did they shake off the secularizing spell it had thrown over them. The earliest prophets — Elijah, Joel, Amos — have nothing to say of the ideal kingdom, nor of its ruler. They speak of deliverance from present distresses, and they admonish the people regarding the causes of these distresses, but the name and work of the Messiah are not once alluded to. But from the middle of the eighth century—from the days of Micah and Isaiah—such allusions are frequent, and gradually the character of Messiah's kingdom is defined with greater exactness, and even the manner in which He is to win it is significantly indicated. That the dominion of the Messiah was destined to be universal, and that a spiritual religion was to characterize the times of the Messiah, these two truths were much insisted on ; and ultimately—possibly after the nation had learned that the truest glory can only be won by suffering, and that the servant of all is the most powerful ruler—it was at first dimly, but with growing emphasis and clearness, disclosed that the Messiah's path to His universal dominion lay through mysterious and unparalleled suffering.

Now, as we look through the prophets to discover what they say about the Messiah, we come to see that in some passages they speak with much greater explicitness of His person and of His work than they do in others. There are passages in which no figure but that of the Messiah was present to the mind of the prophet; there are others in which the figure most prominent in the mind of the prophet is the contemporary king, but such language is applied to him as inevitably suggests the ideal King of Israel. We have thus two classes of Messianic prophecy—a directly and an indirectly Messianic.

(*a*) **Directly Messianic Prophecies.**—There are prophecies in which the prophet spoke directly, and without intervening type or figure, of the coming Messiah. There was present to his mind only the one figure. There was no double reference in his words, first to one person and then to another ; there was but one object before his mind, and one reference in his words. Of this class of prophecies Zechariah furnishes one or two instances, *e.g.* (chap. ix. 9): "Rejoice greatly, O daughter of Zion ; shout, O daughter of Jerusalem : behold, thy King cometh unto thee: He is just, and having salvation; lowly, and riding upon an ass, and upon a colt the foal of an ass." Again (chap. xii. 10): "They shall look upon me whom they have pierced, and they shall mourn for *Him*, as one mourneth for his only son." These passages are generally easy of interpretation to us, although the prophets themselves must often have felt that there was that in their words which they could not wholly understand. They were led by their own utterances to "inquire and search diligently, searching what, or what manner of time, the Spirit which was in them did signify, when it testified beforehand the sufferings of Christ, and the glory that should follow." But that which was obscure to them the event has made plain to us. And it is that which was plainest to them which alone presents any difficulty to us. For in looking at the Messiah, they saw Him through the atmosphere of their own time, and in describing Him they used terms which were familiar to their contemporaries, and conveyed distinct ideas to them, but which to us seem antiquated, and at first sight even contradicted by the actual appearance and work of the Messiah.

An example will illustrate what is meant. In Zech. xiv. 16 the Messianic times are predicted in language which can only apply to them. Nothing else is present to the mind of the prophet. And yet this is the language he uses: "It shall come to pass, that every one that is left of all the nations which come against Jerusalem shall even go up from year to year to worship the King, the Lord of hosts, and to keep the feast of tabernacles." The idea which the prophet wishes to convey is the universality of the Messiah's kingdom, but in his mind this idea is inseparably connected with the external manifestation of submission to Jehovah which was prevalent in his day—coming up to Jerusalem to worship. It was nothing to the prophet that universal acknowledgment of Jehovah would make this outward exhibition of it physically impossible; it was nothing to him that long pilgrimages are attended with abuses and disadvantages far outweighing the advantage of a visible representation of the union of all races: there was no question in his mind about these matters; he only wished to convey the impression that eventually there would be one universal religion, and he represented this idea in terms readily intelligible to his contemporaries. His prediction has not been fulfilled in the letter. The coming of the Messiah did not erect Jerusalem into a local centre for the worship of Jehovah; on the contrary, it was the signal for the superseding of all locally-determined worship. But to hesitate on this account to declare the prophecy fulfilled, were to refuse payment of a debt in sovereigns because it had been contracted in dollars.

The prophets, then, even when consciously speaking of the Messiah, used language which was borrowed from their own time; so that, while the essential reality they predicted was fulfilled by Christ and in Him, the outward form in which they spoke of it was often disregarded. For, to use the weighty words of one who speaks with authority on such points, "prophecy is not history written beforehand, but it has a historical fulfilment. It is truth of the perfect kingdom of God expressed in the forms of life and thinking of O. T. times. But to deny the permanence of the truth on account of the transitoriness of the form, or to affirm the permanence of the form because of the unchangeableness of the truth, either proceeding is about equal to the other in perversity."[1]

(*b*) **Indirectly Messianic Prophecies.** — Besides those passages in which the prophet aimed solely at depicting the Messiah, there are many passages in which the prophet seems to have in view the reigning monarch of his own day, while yet the language he uses does not find a perfect fulfilment save in the Messiah. The kingdom of Israel being the kingdom of God upon earth, and the king being the representative of God, the hope that a divine power, righteousness, and glory would be manifested in the king, must have been continually suggested to all believing men. It was to be expected that this divine background would at all times shine through the present actual reign; that with each accession to the throne the loyalty of the people would tend to depict the actual in the bright colours of the ideal; and that as each reign in succession failed to realize it, the people would take refuge in the future, and more tenaciously than ever cling to the ideal kingdom. These

[1] Professor Davidson in the *Expositor* for October 1878.

aspirations and hopes find utterance through psalmist and prophet, who, as they inaugurate a new era of promise or herald a prince to the throne, do so in terms which are drawn from the ideal king and the ideal kingdom. These utterances, only partially realized in the rulers who first evoked them, find an adequate fulfilment in Him in whom God at last does reign upon earth. That which all previous kings had suggested, either by contrast or by some degree of resemblance, our Lord once for all embodied and made actual in His own person.

Interpretation of Prophecy. — These views of the nature, object, and varieties of prophecy must materially affect our ideas of how we should interpret it. To interpret prophecy has at no time been found easy. Even after all has been done that can be done in the way of accurate translation and historical illustration, there remains a permanent residuum of obscurity. The difficulty experienced by the Ethiopian treasurer is felt by us all : "Of whom speaketh the prophet this? of himself, or of some other man?" And in order to solve this difficulty we commonly ask ourselves one or other of two questions—we ask, What person or event was it possible or probable that the prophet had in view when he uttered such and such words? or we ask, What person or event satisfies the terms of the prophecy? But it is obvious that neither of these questions alone will give us the true key to the predictions. The first does not, because there are many prophecies in which it is plain that the prophet had primarily in view some person or event of his own time; and yet the language he uses regarding it is so grand as to seem extravagant if the application be confined to these contemporary events or persons. The language, *e.g.*, of the second Psalm is undoubtedly applicable to David; but when we come to the verse: "The Lord hath said unto me, Thou art my Son; this day have I begotten Thee. I will give Thee the uttermost parts of the earth as Thy possession," we feel that in such expressions the pride even of oriental monarchs is outdone, and that the language is either ridiculously extravagant or finds an application in some other and greater monarch than David. It was David idealized that was spoken of. We at once, then, find this to be an insufficient clue to the interpretation of prophecy, to ask what the prophet had in view when he uttered it. Besides, Peter assures us (1 Pet. i. 10) that though the prophets spoke with confidence and with intelligence, yet they did not themselves always see the full significance of their words. They felt sure that certain things would come to pass, but when or how they could not say. And we who live in the times of fulfilment can see in their words a meaning which it is impossible they could have fully seen.

On the other hand, we get an equally insufficient answer if we ask, What person or event adequately fulfils such and such a prophecy? Because to understand a prophecy or any other intelligent utterance, we must look at it from the speaker's point of view, and in connection with the circumstances which called it forth. Now, the prophet uniformly spoke to his contemporaries, and *primarily* for their sake. And he spoke to them not that he might gratify an idle curiosity about occurrences which were to take place long after they had been removed from earth, but that he might give them sufficient light and inducement to bear up against present calamities, and to play their own part well in that continuous history which was running on through them to glorious events. He spoke of the future as it was connected with and to be evolved out of the present. He saw the future through the present, and as its outcome. And consequently he saw it in the *terms* of the present.

There is, in short, a double reference in prophecy, as there is a double authorship. Throughout the whole system of revelation there are two intelligences at work—the originating, guiding, and informing mind of God; and the intelligent, prepared, and co-operating human mind. The prophet speaks intelligently. He does not merely make articulate sounds which have no root in his own mind and will. He utters what he has himself thought [heard] and perceived. At the same time, he does not see all the connections of what he utters with the future of God's kingdom. These are visible only to the infinite mind that foresees the end from the beginning, and that is guiding all things towards the designed consummation. The prophet announces that "The Lord shall dwell with His people;" but his view of this dwelling, if not limited by the divine inhabitation of the temple, yet falls far short of the incarnation which really fulfilled his prediction. The prophet saw this *principle* of the kingdom of God, and declared that it would be realized; but the precise form in which it was destined to be realized he did not see. Or, again, Malachi predicts that the Lord shall suddenly come to His temple and purify it so as to provide a pure worship for Himself; but there is no evidence that he had any idea either of the how or the when, as Peter says, either of the time or the manner in which this was to be done. Here, again, this *principle* of the kingdom of God, that He will secure a cleansed and pure worship, is firmly grasped by the prophet; but the form in which this principle will be perfectly realized is not seen by him, but only by God. No doubt there are some prophecies in which both time and manner are foretold by the prophet, but these are very few in proportion.

The interpreter of prophecy must accordingly keep these two meanings distinct in his own mind.[1] He must distinguish between the meaning which was obvious to the prophet himself, and that fulfilment which the supernaturally-guided evolution of events, and especially of the kingdom of God upon earth, gave to his words. And from this double reference of prophecy it obviously results that the words of the prophet may be expected frequently to fail of any literal fulfilment, that precise state of things under which he lived and prophesied having passed entirely away. A large number of predictions never have been and never can be fulfilled in the letter, the kingdom of God has come not in that precise form which was predicted, but the expectations of the prophets have been realized in even higher forms than they looked for. The same principle is found running through God's dealings with the individual. "God's promises," says Dr. Bruce, "are never delusive, though they may be illusive." A promise, and the hope or prospect it begets, lead a man to make attainment which lifts him to a higher level and makes

---

[1] "The prophets will never come to their rights, nor be recognised as the men of power and individuality which they were, unless we carefully distinguish between prophecy—that is, what the prophets in their own day and circumstances themselves meant—and fulfilment—that is, the shape in which the principles of the kingdom of God which they enunciated will, amidst the enormous changes that have passed over the form of that kingdom and of the world, find their final realization" (Professor Davidson in the *Expositor*, October 1878).

him superior to its fulfilment. "Dig deep over all my ground," said the dying father to his sons, "and you will find much gold." They found no pots of gold as they expected, but they fell in love with honest labour, and their land was permanently improved by the digging and abundantly enriched them. "In the regeneration," said our Lord to His disciples, "ye shall sit upon twelve thrones judging the twelve tribes of Israel." And probably from these words the apostles gathered that our Lord meant to establish a tribal government in the land, and that as any successful general appoints his most serviceable officers to the government of conquered districts, so should they have their several provinces. This hope was enough for the apostles as they then were, and by the help of it they grew up into a mature condition in which they would have felt such a reward to be paltry and disappointing. So does all prophecy, by speaking to its own generation in terms it can understand, and appealing to its hopes by symbols it appreciates, lead the Church of God hopefully and faithfully onwards to a growth and a future worthy of its Lord.

Permanent Uses of Prophecy.—1. Ethical Function.—The uses of prophecy did not terminate with its fulfilment. Its ethical value remains. The writings of the prophets, enforcing as they do the permanent principles and constant laws of the kingdom of God, are profitable in every age of that kingdom's history. It is in these recorded prophecies that we hear the very counsel which God saw to be fit as He watched the growth of His people age by age, standing by them in all dangers, in all weaknesses, in all distresses. It is in them we have that very instrument whereby God maintained the existence of His people for many generations, and it is by using it for our own maintenance and life that we learn its value, and that nothing else can take its place. No part of Scripture sheds such direct light on experience; none so follows the soul through all the windings of a God-forgetting, worldly, embittered, repentant, God-seeking life; none so meets and appeals to the soul in every emergency, and has the right word to say to every variety of feeling.

2. Evidential Function.—It is much more difficult to estimate the value of prophecy as an evidence of religion. The argument from prophecy is one form of the argument from miracles, and is subject to the same limitations as that argument. It is, *e.g.*, insufficient to prove the existence of a Personal God. We can at the best merely show that prophecy introduces us to phenomena in human history which are inexplicable on any known law of human nature, and which would be explained on the hypothesis that there is such a Being as God. We must assume the existence of God. But even with this assumption, the argument from prophecy is one which it is very difficult to conduct, and which may very easily be over-strained. There is, however, validity in it, and practically many have felt its force. Indeed, at first sight, the argument deducible from prophecy in favour of Christianity as a divinely-given religion would seem to be irresistible. Experience, however, has taught apologists to assign to it, as well as to the *general* argument from miracles, a somewhat less prominent place than they once occupied. And perhaps the tendency at present is to make too little rather than too much of this line of defence.

The true relation of these subordinate evidences to the self-evidencing power of all revelation is given by our Lord Himself in His words to Philip (John xiv. 9–11) : "Have I been so long time with you, and yet hast thou not known me, Philip? . . . Believe me that I am in the Father, and the Father in me : or else believe me for the very works' sake." That is to say, our Lord expected that "they that were of the truth" would hear His voice, that God would be manifested through His flesh to those who had eyes to see ; but yet if this first and strongest evidence should fail, then those who had no eye for the higher marks of divinity in the love, truth, and graciousness of Christ's person, might be aroused to listen to His voice by the miracles which He did (comp. John viii. 18 and x. 37, 38).

This superiority of the self-evidencing power of Christ's person and life to all other evidences, is also affirmed by the common experience of Christians. There is a faith which cannot be called intellectual, and which perhaps cannot give much reason for itself, but which is yet stronger, sounder, and more fruitful than the faith which is produced by a consideration of evidences. The faith of a child in its mother is unintelligent, and cannot render a reason ; and it is this faith which Christ sets in our midst as the pattern faith. A true nature intuitively accepts the truth. Therefore our Lord often showed Himself disappointingly careless about external proofs and credentials of His mission, denying to those who had asked from Him any sign which did not naturally occur in the course of life to which love and holiness called Him, and contenting Himself with some such saying as, "Every one that is of the truth heareth my voice." To a man who has open eyes, it is out of place to prove the presence of light; neither need you tell a man that some article of food is useless or unwholesome if he has lived and thriven upon it unto this day. Most persons who believe in Christ do so because they are conscious of a suitableness between what they need and what He provides. Love can rarely justify itself, and is confounded when asked for a reason. It is the whole nature that believes, not the understanding alone or first. It is a man's life and habits and natural disposition which quicken or retard his faith, as well as his reading and thinking.

Still, though the evidence furnished by miracles and prophecy is not of the highest kind, it ought not on that account to be overlooked. If it cannot always produce faith, it may sometimes preserve it from decaying. If not the nourishment of faith, it may at least serve as its medicine. No man would think to improve his walk by wearing splints, but he finds their use if he breaks his leg. And there are times of weakened faith, and of slow, dull spiritual life, when, were it not for these much-maligned evidences, we might lose our hold upon God and things spiritual altogether.

From a consideration of our Lord's fixed habit, then, and also from a consideration of the nature of faith, we see that neither miracles nor prophecy can stand in the first line of defence. The same result is reached if we consider the nature of prophecy. For every one who peruses the writings of the prophets is at once struck with the large proportion which the moral and spiritual teaching bears to the predictive matter. Indeed, he soon becomes aware that prediction occupies a secondary place, and is commonly introduced in the shape of warning or encouragement, in order to give weight and effect to the moral teaching. Some of the greatest of the prophets, such as

Samuel and Elijah, uttered scarcely any predictions at all; while those uttered by Moses, the prophet most comparable to our Lord Himself, bear a very small proportion to his other teaching. We miss the meaning of prophecy, therefore, and we quite misunderstand the function of the Israelitish prophet, if we measure its importance merely or mainly by the insight it gives into the future. As Aaron is called the "prophet" of Moses because he was to be his mouthpiece or spokesman, so every one whom God sent to speak for Him, to reveal His will or enforce it, was a prophet. The prophets were God's messengers, not appearing at stated intervals, but when an emergency made a voice from heaven desirable; not the regular product of any national institution, and so bound to partake in the national corruption, but coming from outside the world's clamour with counsel men felt to be divine. The prophets formed a line of inspired advisers and censors of morals; able in every emergency to give the right direction; foreseeing when the enemies of Israel should be resisted, and when submission was necessary; enlightened to put the right interpretation on every national disaster; commissioned to recall the people from all backsliding, to repress prevalent vice, to alarm the formalists and the immoral, and to disclose an encouraging future to the faithful. God was revealing Himself in the history of Israel, and the prophets were sent to guide the history towards its determined end, to shed light on all God's dealings with the people, and guide them forward step by step. It was through the prophecy running alongside of the history, as well as through the history itself, that God did in point of fact make Himself known. It is therefore true, as Rothe says, that prophecy is no mere adjunct of revelation, attached to it from without in order to prove it to us, but is itself a constituent part of revelation.

It will, then, be apparent that there are two views which may be taken of the relation in which the predictive element in prophecy stands to its ethical contents, and it will also be apparent which of these views is the more correct. It is clear that the prophets were sent chiefly for the sake of guiding the people to a knowledge of their duty, and stimulating them to its performance, and only in so far as a knowledge of the future was helpful towards these ends did they disclose the future. This knowledge of the future was imparted to them, not always that they might by this miraculous foreknowledge authenticate their mission, but always that by the prospect of good or evil to come the people might be quickened to obey their message. As the miracles of our Lord found their occasion in some genuine need of persons who appealed to His compassion, and were never mere signs and wonders[1] done merely for the sake of showing His power, as He positively and even with indignation refused to leap off the pinnacle of the temple, and, by lighting uninjured in the court below, give evidence of His superhuman power, so the prophetic utterances were all called forth by some contemporaneous and genuine emergency. The view given of the future was conditioned by that emergency, and however far-reaching was the truth delivered, it had its root in the present distress. But this does not prevent prophecy from having any evidential value. The primary object, no doubt, was ethical, but a subordinate purpose was at the same time served. The primary object of a poet is to give utterance to the thoughts that burn in his brain. He does not aim at being recognised as a poet; but none the less does this result follow. The charitable man has no craving for applause when he gives alms, and precisely in so far as his primary object is to be known as charitable is he really lacking in charity. But although his primary object is to relieve the distress that has come under his notice, this does not prevent his benevolence from exerting an evidential function in the way of proving that he is a charitable person. Thus also the primary object of our Lord's miracles was to relieve distress, but they none the less served an evidential purpose. Prophecy, too, had for its primary object to guide God's people through contemporaneous difficulties, but this need not prevent it from serving a secondary object. The prophets may *so* guide the people as to convey the distinct impression that their minds are supernaturally enlightened.

But we can safely go a step farther than this, and claim for the predictive element in prophecy an explicit and intended evidential value, *at least in some instances.* The fulfilment of prediction is laid

---

[1] Possibly the cursing of the fig-tree and the finding of the stater in the fish's mouth are exceptions.

down in Deuteronomy (chap. xviii. 21) as the simple test by which the true and the false prophet might be distinguished : "If thou say in thine heart, How shall we know the word which the Lord hath not spoken ? When a prophet speaketh in the name of the Lord, if the thing follow not, nor come to pass, that is the thing which the Lord hath not spoken, but the prophet hath spoken it presumptuously : thou shalt not be afraid of him." And in Jeremiah's time we find that this same test was popularly accepted as sufficient, and truth in prediction was reckoned a guarantee that the prophet was commissioned by God (comp. Jer. xxviii. 9). And something of the same kind is involved in the words of our Lord to His apostles : "Now I have told you before it come to pass, that, when it is come to pass, ye might believe" (John xiv. 29 ; comp. xiii. 19 and xvi. 4 : in the latter passage our Lord has a different object in view, and not a strictly evidential one). Matthew Arnold speaks with a kind of contemptuous pity of those who need external evidences. "It must," he says (*Lit. and Dogma*, p. 113), "be allowed, that while human nature is what it is, the mass of men are likely to listen more to a teacher of righteousness if he accompanies his teaching by an exhibition of supernatural prescience." Certainly ; and if the revelation of God is to be a revelation at all, it must be progressive, beginning with men at the beginning and going on step by step ; and if it is progressive, then it must necessarily in its earliest parts adapt itself to man's earliest stage, and speak to him in terms he can understand, and convince him by proof suited to his capacity. As, therefore, Moses received power from God to work *signs* before Pharaoh, as well as the plagues which were primarily judgments and incidentally signs ; so were the prophets, when occasion required, empowered to work *signs* of supernatural prescience in confirmation of their message, as well as to see the future in its moral bearing upon the condition of the people with whom they had to do. It were surprising if we found that the same evidences which we require had been used to convince those who lived in the world's infancy ; but it were also surprising if, on the other hand, we found that the evidences which were largely relied upon by the apostles were wholly invalid.

In using prophecy for evidential purposes, it becomes apparent that there are certain classes of prophecies of which we cannot avail ourselves.

1. There are, in the first place, those predictions of which we cannot with confidence affirm that, in order to make them, supernatural enlightenment was required. As Bacon says: "Probable conjectures [or obscure traditions] many times turn themselves into prophecies." It is quite certain that in the early years of Rome, the duration of that great power was limited by augury to twelve centuries. It is within the memory of many now alive that the recent civil war in America was foretold, and even the time of its occurrence definitely predicted. A remarkable prediction of the Sikh war may be found in Robertson's *History of India*. And considering that there is no exercise of mind to which men are more addicted than that of forecasting the future, and considering that since ever the world began men have indulged in prediction at the risk of their reputation for wisdom, it cannot appear surprising that one guess in each thousand years should be so remarkably true as to be remembered. It would contradict the law of chances if some out of so large a number of guesses had not come true.

But besides happy guesses, there are readings of the future of a more certain kind. Any one can predict the fall of a stone which has been thrown into the air; and the physician can foretell the course of a disease, the various steps in its progress, and its result. The statesman who has given his attention to the history of nations may acquire great skill in forecasting their future, and may see laws or principles at work which predict to him either the decay or the increased prosperity of the country to which he belongs. Attempts are in our own day being made to reduce all social and political matters to a science, so that as the chemist can predict the result of certain combinations, or the meteorologist warn the fishermen all round the coast of a coming storm, the politician or the citizen may be able to predict the future of his nation, and the result of every act of government and social movement. Whether this science will overtake all that its somewhat boastful programme sketches, and accomplish its great design, is doubtful in the extreme. At all events, the results of this science are still in the future.

However, we must beware of using, as evidence of supernatural enlightenment, predictions which may really be within the reach of reasonable conjecture or keen human insight, cultivated and instructed by long experience. It might, *e.g.*, be difficult to prove that our Lord's prediction of His own death required a supernatural knowledge. To a man like Gamaliel, it might have been clear from the first that such a career could end in nothing else. And it may, *in many particular instances* of O. T. prophecy, be impossible to prove that in predicting the prosperity of Israel or the downfall of her enemies, the prophets were doing anything more than making reasonable deductions from the uniform principles on which, as they believed, the world is governed. It is impossible, that is to say, to convince, by such instances, any one who is not previously disposed to be convinced, that the prophets had any supernatural prescience. If these instances are taken one by one, it is always possible for a man, whose leaning is towards a naturalistic interpretation of all such phenomena, to find a way of explaining the correspondence between the prediction and its fulfilment without supposing any supernatural control. It is always open to him to say: This event to which you point me as a fulfilment of prophecy might have been foreseen by any one who believed that national acts have national consequences for good or evil.

2. A second class of prophecies, of which we cannot avail ourselves for evidential purposes, consists of those which suggested their own fulfilment. A familiar instance of this is the announcement made by the witches to Macbeth. This prophecy fulfilled itself by suggesting to the ambitious spirit of Macbeth a higher preferment than he might otherwise have thought of; and when once there sank into his mind the impression that this was his destiny, he immediately gave all his energies to the work of accomplishing it. And it is quite conceivable that any patriotic Jew, who was smitten with the ambition of delivering his people, should have been prompted by O. T. prophecy to assume some of the marks of the Messiah, and thus apparently fulfil the prophecies. It is notorious that attempts have been made to explain the whole life of Jesus Himself on a similar principle. It has been affirmed, either

that Jesus Himself was guided in the formation of His career by O. T. prophecy, or that His followers ascribed to Him actions which, though not actually done by Him, seemed to them necessary to justify His claim to be the Messiah.

The little fragment of truth to be derived from this proposed method of construing the life of Christ is simply this, that any action of Christ's which was so slight and insignificant and easy that any one might have done it, cannot be pleaded evidentially as a fulfilment of prophecy, even though it is in exact correspondence with ancient prediction. But, on the other hand, we must beware of giving up too much; for some fulfilments of prophecy in the life of our Lord are not so external and barely symbolic as they seem. It might at first appear, *e.g.*, as if nothing could be easier than to fulfil Zechariah's most explicit prophecy of the Messiah, by riding into Jerusalem on an ass. But to ride into a city on an ass is one thing, to ride in amid the enthusiastic acclamations of the people as the acknowledged king is quite another thing. Any man could do the former, but the latter could only be brought about by one who had gained ascendancy over the popular imagination, if not over the human heart—that is to say, only by one who already possessed one of the prime qualifications for the Messianic office. And even though Christ did this or other actions with the conscious and expressed design of fitting prophecy with its fulfilment, even though it be shown that in these actions He played the *rôle* of the Messiah as it was indicated in the O. T.,[1] yet it remains to be explained how He, and no one else who had equal access to these prophecies, was able to fulfil them.

And it should be observed in this connection, that if designed coincidences can have no direct evidential value, undesigned coincidences have a weight proportioned to the unlikelihood and difficulty of their occurrence. If no weight can be attached to a fulfilment so easy that any one, if so minded, could accomplish it; great weight must be attached to those fulfilments which the very

[1] "It has long been manifest that the chief *literal* fulfilment by Jesus Christ of things said by the prophets was the fulfilment such as would naturally be given by one who nourished his spirit on the prophets, and on living and acting their words" (*Lit. and Dogma*, p. 118).

men who were destined to accomplish them would have striven against and by all means sought to avoid. Had it occurred to the priests who bought the worked-out brick-field or clay-hole in which Judas had committed suicide, that, so far from finding a clever way of disposing of the price of blood which was burning their hands, they were actually fulfilling Zechariah's prophecy to their own permanent confusion, and furnishing one more link of proof in favour of the claims of Jesus, they would certainly have done whatever lay in their power to prevent this fulfilment.

3. A third class of passages which it seems unwise to use for evidential purposes are those which may feasibly be explained as merely forming the necessary poetical drapery of the central idea in the prophet's mind. When, *e.g.*, Zephaniah wishes to depict vividly the desolation of Nineveh, he naturally draws from a poetic fancy those characteristic marks of desolation which would best convey the idea; and he says: "The cormorant and the bittern shall lodge in the upper lintels of it; their voice shall sing in the windows." But if a bittern should happen to rise from a lintel while a Christian apologist is passing, this itself is not, strictly speaking, a fulfilment of prophecy, any more than we could fairly say that the prophecy was not fulfilled if neither cormorant nor other quiet-loving fowl made its appearance. Both assailants and advocates of the supernatural in prophecy seem to have erred at this point: the assailants denying the fulfilment of a prophecy where the mere poetical accessories have been unfulfilled, and the advocates making so much of these mere details of imagery as to provoke and unsettle the faith of men disposed to believe. Books which have gone too far in pressing the fulfilment of these insignificant details, have given a great opportunity to the assailants of the faith, who expose, and find it easy to expose, the incompetency of this line of argument, and turn away the attention of inquirers from the essential contents of prophecy, or prejudice the mind against it.

At the same time, there are details which cannot with certainty be accounted mere drapery, and there are some which certainly cannot be so accounted. When Nahum, in depicting the downfall of Nineveh, declares that the fire shall devour her, little weight can be attached to this. When he says, "With an overrunning flood he will make an end of the place thereof," it may fairly be maintained that this is something more than needful drapery, or a mere figure of speech, although an opposite opinion may find a good deal to say for itself; but when the prophet adds that the city shall be taken "while they are drunken as drunkards," it is felt to be somewhat forced to explain away this detail also as mere natural imagery. Similarly, when we find Ezekiel predicting (chap. xii. 13) not only the captivity but the blindness of Zedekiah, this detail must be accepted as evidence of supernatural foresight, unless it can be shown that the putting out of the eyes of captive princes was a regular custom among the Chaldæans. Or, when Jeremiah does not content himself with predicting the untimely death of the false prophet Hananiah, but expressly says (chap. xxviii. 16), "*This year* thou shalt die," the fulfilment of this prediction may fairly be considered as evidence of a foresight not explicable on any known law of the human mind.

But the strength of the argument from prophecy lies not in particular instances of superficial or profound harmony betwen prediction and fulfilment, but in the scope and fulfilment of prophecy as a whole. What we have here to do with is not a few scattered prognostications or happy guesses, but a coherent series or system of utterances extending throughout the entire pre-Christian history of our race. The phenomenon we have to account for is that of a series of men, each claiming to be God's messenger, and certainly speaking the truth of God, each adding to what his predecessors had uttered, and all agreeing in predicting an end and consummation so strange that their words were neither wholly understood nor believed, and which yet was eventually realized, and when realized proved to be the most important epoch in the history of our race.[1] There can be no doubt that on this line of Hebrew prophecy, and on this line alone, men continued from first to last persistently to look for the salvation of God. It matters not to the argument whether this or that particular prediction be fulfilled; it matters not whether it be true or not that, as Matthew Arnold affirms, many of

[1] See *The Argument from Prophecy*, by Brownlow Maitland, p. 27.

the applications of prophecy to Christ are "based on a mere unintelligent catching at the letter of the O. T., isolated from its context and real meaning;"[1] there remains the undeniable fact that the hope of God's redemption, and of Him who was to accomplish it, was developed from age to age with increasing definiteness by this line of men. No one can read the prophets without being persuaded that at least in three great particulars they did truly foretell Christian times. They had a full persuasion that the worship of Jehovah would one day cease to be national and become universal, that it would cease to be outward and ceremonial and become spiritual, and that the kingdom of God would one day be established upon earth by a personal ruler with whom as time went on they somehow connected the idea of suffering. To use the words of one[2] who has given this subject a careful treatment: "We are then shut up to this account of the case, that out of Hebrew prophecy, which flowed like a mighty stream through many ages, ever gaining in volume and strength, there emerged at least three great and true forecasts of the future of religion and of God's dealings with the world, of such a kind as to indicate the presence and activity of some informing element which was not native to the national mind and genius; and that these forecasts prepared the way for, and were afterwards realized in, the wonderful rise and spread of Christianity, which in its world-wide catholicity, its lofty spirituality, and its doctrine of salvation through the passion and exaltation of its Divine Founder, fulfilled all the expectations which the prophets had long before expressed, yet in a manner which transcended the mere letter of their predictions, and was more in accordance with the highest reality and the most universal truth than any barely literal accomplishment could have been."

[1] *Literature and Dogma*, p. 156:
[2] Brownlow Maitland, *Argument*, p. 186.

INTRODUCTION

TO

THE BOOK OF HAGGAI.

OF the prophets who lived after the captivity, or, as they are sometimes called, the Prophets of the Restoration, Haggai[1] was the earliest. But of his history nothing is known save what may be gathered from his own brief prophecies, and from the allusions to his work which are found in the fifth and sixth chapters of the book of Ezra. It has been conjectured, from his reference to the first temple (chap. ii. 3), that he himself had seen it. With greater probability the Psalms numbered in our version as the 146th, 147th, 148th, and 149th have been attributed to him and Zechariah; although the fact that the names of these prophets occur in the superscription of these Psalms may only indicate that they were introduced into the temple service on their recommendation.[2] But though so little is known of the man, his work was of great importance. No prophet ever appeared at a more critical juncture in the history of the people, and, it may be added, no prophet was more immediately successful.

[1] The name "Haggai" is said by Gesenius to be an adjective formed from *Hag*, a feast. It would thus be the Hebrew equivalent of the Roman name *Festus*, and akin to the Greek *Hilary*. This mode of forming proper names was not unusual among the Hebrews, *e.g. Barzillai* = a man of iron, from *Barzel* = iron. Dr. Pusey, however, thinks it an abbreviated form of Haggiah, a name which is found in 1 Chron. vi. 30, and means *festival of Jehovah*. The word *Hag* (from *hagag*, to whirl round in a circle, or dance, and hence to keep a feast) is the term in Arabic appropriated by Moslems to denote the caravan of pilgrims to Mecca, or a single pilgrim (comp. the Jewish pilgrimages to their annual feasts, Lev. xxiii. 41). It is pronounced *hadj* except in Egypt. Why had Haggai's parents given him this name? Was he born on the day of some feast?

[2] In the case of the 138th Psalm the reading is doubtful, and the internal evidence adverse.

The circumstances which seemed urgent enough to call for divine interference at this time were as follows. The capture of Babylon by Cyrus, and the consequent amalgamation of the kingdom of Assyria with the Persian empire, materially affected the fortunes of the Jews. "Of all the Persian monarchs, Cyrus was the one most distinguished for mildness and clemency; the one to whom the sufferings of a captive nation, torn violently from its home and subjected to seventy years of grievous oppression, would most forcibly have appealed. Again, he was an earnest Zoroastrian, a worshipper of the 'Great God Ormazd,' . . he was a hater of idolatry, and of the shameless rites which accompanied it, and he would naturally sympathize with such a people as the Jews—a people whose religious views bore so great a resemblance to his own. Thus the restoration of the Jews by Cyrus, though an act almost without a parallel in the history of the world, was only natural under the circumstances."[1] By whatever motives prompted, Cyrus issued a decree [B.C. 536] permitting the captive Jews to return to their own country. But it is not always easy for expatriated men to abandon their adopted homes. The majority of the Jews preferred to remain in exile, having acquired properties[2] and positions which they found themselves unable to resign. These exiles were afterwards known as "the Dispersion," and exercised considerable influence in various ways. Under Zerubbabel, the representative of David's line, and Joshua the high priest, there returned to Judæa 42,360 men with their families and some thousands of slaves.[3] They arrived in early spring, and were welcomed by those Jews who had been living in their own land. Barely a year elapsed before preparations had been made for the rebuilding of the temple, and in the second month of the second year of the return, the foundation-stone was laid. Speedily, however, the work was interrupted by the jealousy of the Samaritans, who continued during the reigns of Cyrus and Cambyses[4] to misrepresent the Jews at the court of Persia; and at last obtained from Smerdis (who was a Magian) an edict forbidding

[1] Rawlinson, *Illustrations of O. T.* Daniel's position, too, influenced Cyrus.
[2] If the statement of Haman (Esther iii. 9) is a safe basis of calculation, the property of the Jews of the dispersion in his time must have exceeded £4,000,000, not, as Dr. Pusey miscalculates, £300,000,000.
[3] Probably over 200,000 souls altogether.
[4] Apparently called Ahasuerus in Ezra iv. 6. "The Hebrew *Ahashverosh* is the exact Semitic equivalent of the Persian *Khshayarsha*, which the Greeks rendered by Xerxes" (Rawlinson, *Illustrations*, p. 191). He thinks Cambyses was known to some of his subjects under the name of Xerxes.

the work of restoration to go on (Ezra iv. 7-24). The tide again turned when Darius Hystaspis[1] came to the throne. Trusting to his known sympathies, the prophets Haggai and Zechariah roused the people and their chief to renew the work of rebuilding the city and the temple. Animated by their appeals and promises, Zerubbabel and the people gave themselves again to the work, and eventually completed the temple, which was dedicated in the sixth year of Darius (B.C. 516).

The men who take the initiative in a national crisis such as this, must have words to utter which are at once suitable to the occasion, and fitted to penetrate to the springs of action in men's hearts and consciences. It is never an easy task to persuade a whole population to make pecuniary sacrifices, to postpone private to public interests; and the probability is, that in these brief remains of the prophet Haggai we have but one or two specimens of a ceaseless diligence and persistent determination, which upheld and animated the whole people till the work was accomplished. The return from exile had its dark as well as its bright side. It was a kind of new birth, a second exodus, a great era from which the history of the nation might be expected to start with a cleansed path and revived hope and purpose. "The exile corresponds in the history of the Israelitish people with that epoch in the life of man when, after many storms, and tumults, and sorrowful wanderings, he passes from the illusions of youth to the calm maturity of manhood."[2] But, as in the individual life, the chastened penitent, purified as his spirit may be, has in some cases no longer the material or the physical means of showing what this life should be; so this nation, purged as it was from the causes of its banishment, had yet lost its opportunity for some purposes, and henceforth drags out a poor and insignificant career in great part unrecorded and with scarcely one great name to the century.

The results of the captivity in the character and habits of the people have been thus epitomized:—"Before the captivity they were continually sliding into idolatry, afterwards they hated it with a fanatical hatred. Before, they hankered after kingly rule; afterwards, they became, contrary to the usual course of history, submissive to priestly authority. Before, they neglected the written word; afterwards, they regarded it with a superstitious reverence that was well-nigh idolatrous. Before, they were continually forming alliances with foreign nations; afterwards, they regarded all other nations

---

[1] Darius Hystaspis, *i.e.* Darius, son of Hystaspes.
[2] Reuss, *Apostolic Age*, i. 40.

with a contemptuous abhorrence. Before, they were eminently an agricultural people; afterwards, they became, what they still are, a trading people." The influences which produced some at least of these results are not difficult to detect. The most striking change was the absolute abandonment of idolatry, a result which would naturally follow not only from their consideration of the causes of the miseries which had befallen them, but also from their observation of the impotence of idols in all practical matters, and from their contact with the conquering iconoclastic monotheist, Cyrus. Again, it was in separation from their land and temple that the Jews as a people could first learn the comparative value of local services and spiritual worship; as it was also in these circumstances they were led to lean not upon obvious material privileges as the guarantee of God's favour and calling, but upon His word that could be listened to on the banks of the river Chebar as well as in the streets of Jerusalem. Hence the synagogues and their worship, and all the important alterations in Jewish society which went hand in hand with this great innovation. Once more, it was as fellow-sufferers that the tribes at last learned to forget their divisions and jealousies. Under the pressure of common misfortune, they were once again welded and compacted into one people. As the sons of Jacob had to be sent into Egypt to learn among other things that they were one family distinct from others, and to acquire at least as much brotherly feeling as would prevent them from selling one another, so, after the return, we read no longer of fratricidal wars and a divided nation.

Contents.—The prophecies of Haggai are dated with unusual precision, and are therefore very easily distinguished from one another. There are four distinct utterances:—

1. In the first (chap. i. 1-11), Haggai reproaches the people for their neglect of the rebuilding of the temple. The good result of this appeal is narrated in vv. 12-15.

2. In the second (chap. ii. 1-9), delivered about a month after the work had been resumed, he counteracts the disparaging observations the old men had been making on the rising temple.

3. In the third (chap. ii. 10-19), delivered exactly three months after the building had been resumed, he explains to the people why their past prayers had been unanswered, and promises them abundant crops if they go on vigorously with the temple.

4. In the fourth (chap. ii. 20-23), delivered on the same day as the third, ample assurances of support and protection are given to Zerubbabel.

HAGGAI.

CHAPTER I.

1 IN the second year of Darius the king, in the sixth month, in the first day of the month, came the word of the LORD by Haggai the prophet unto Zerubbabel the son of Shealtiel, governor of Judah, and to Joshua the son of Josedech, the 2 high priest, saying, Thus speaketh the LORD of hosts, saying,

THE FIRST PROPHECY (i. 1–15).

Haggai reproaches the people with their neglect of the work of rebuilding the temple, points out to them the evil consequences of this neglect, and moves them to resume the work.

1. *The second year of Darius*, 520 B.C. Darius, son of Hystaspes, reigned over the Persian empire from 521–486 B.C.

The sixth month, *i.e.* of the Jewish ecclesiastical year, beginning with the month Nisan, which most nearly synchronized with our April. The sixth month, Elul, fell therefore about the time of September. The civil year of the Jews began in Tisri (October). In the sixth month the yield of the harvest was already ascertained (ver. 6).

First day of the month. The Jewish months were lunar, extending from one appearing of the new moon to another. The *first day*, being the new moon, was a religious holiday (cp. Amos viii. 5; 2 Kings iv. 23). The people would therefore naturally gather to the sanctuary, and might be more than usually alive to the shame of leaving the temple in ruins. Hence the suitability of the day to the prophet's purpose.

By Haggai, lit. by the hand of Haggai, by Haggai's instrumentality (cp. Ex. iv. 13; Lev. viii. 36; Gal. iii. 19). *Unto Zerubbabel, son of Shealtiel.* According to 1 Chron. iii. 19, he was the son of Pedaiah, a brother of Shealtiel, son of Jeconiah, *i.e.* Jehoiachin. According to Luke iii. 27, he was the son of Shealtiel, son of Neri. To reconcile these statements, it is suggested that Shealtiel may have died childless, and his brother Pedaiah, by levirate marriage with his widow, became the father of Zerubbabel. In like manner Shealtiel himself may have been only the adopted son of Jeconiah (see Jer. xxii. 30). *Governor* is expressed here by the word specially used of the officer appointed by the Persian government, Pechah, a Pasha. The prophet addresses the civil and ecclesiastical representatives of the people.

2. *This people*, not *my people;* there is a touch of reproach in the term. Their excuse, "*the time is not come*," may have been grounded on a calculation

This people say, The time is not come, the time that the LORD's house should be built. Then came the word of the LORD by Haggai the prophet, saying, *Is it* time for you, O ye, to dwell in your ceiled houses, and this house *lie* waste? Now therefore thus saith the LORD of hosts; Consider your ways. Ye have sown much, and bring in little; ye eat, but ye have not enough; ye drink, but ye are not filled with drink; ye clothe you, but there is none warm; and he that earneth wages earneth wages *to put it* into a bag with holes. Thus saith the LORD of hosts; Consider your ways.

of 70 years from the destruction of the temple by Nebuchadnezzar in 586 B.C.[1] But more probably they used the common plea that Providence was obviously against them, bidding them desist by throwing obstacles in their way. Temptations are very commonly courted under the name of Providences.

4. Their own comforts were their condemnation. If they had found means, leisure, and security to furnish such houses for themselves, it could scarcely be the times which prevented them from building God's house. Contrast David's, "See now, I dwell in an house of cedar, but the ark of God dwelleth within curtains." "Surely I will not come into the tabernacle of my house ... until I find out a place for the Lord" (2 Sam. vii. 2; Ps. cxxxii. 3-5). "Our expenditures on ourselves, whilst we pretend to have nothing for God, will bear emphatic and fearful testimony against us" (Moore). Self first and God afterwards, the bulk to self, the parings to God, is the rule with all.

Ceiled means **wainscoted**, *elaborately finished with wood-work*. To *ceil*, like the Hebrew word it stands for, signifies to *cover*, to *overlay*, as with boards or gold. "To *seal* the eyes of a hawk or dove was to sew up their eyelids, and in this sense is used by Shakespeare (*Ant. and Cleop.* iii. 2):

"' But when we in our viciousness grow hard,
(O mercy on't) the wise gods *seal* our eyes.'"

5. *Consider your ways,* lit. **set your heart upon your ways.** Reflect upon your conduct and its results, and you will recognise that the Lord resents your indifference and selfish delay in building. The consequence of our own sin is often our best monitor. "It is the Hebrew phrase for the endeavour, characteristic of the gifted seers of all times, to compel their hearers to turn the inside of their hearts outwards to their own view, to take the masks from off their consciences, to 'see life steadily, and to see it whole'" (Stanley, *Jew. Church*, iii. 101).

6. Nothing had prospered with them. Their harvests were bad; their food did not nourish them, and even the hard cash they hoarded leaked imperceptibly away. It is often observable in a bankrupt's examination that he cannot tell what has become of his money. It happened with the Jews as with the villain in the ballad:

" His barns were fired, his goods consumed,
His lands were barren made,
His cattle died within the field,
And *nothing with him stayed.*"

(Cp. 2 Kings xii. 4-16.)

[1] According to others 588 or 587. Cp. Jer. li.

8 Go up to the mountain, and bring wood, and build the house; and I will take pleasure in it, and I will be glorified, saith
9 the LORD. Ye looked for much, and, lo, *it came* to little; and when ye brought *it* home, I did blow upon it. Why? saith the LORD of hosts. Because of mine house that *is*
10 waste, and ye run every man unto his own house. Therefore the heaven over you is stayed from dew, and the earth is
11 stayed *from* her fruit. And I called for a drought upon the land, and upon the mountains, and upon the corn, and upon the new wine, and upon the oil, and upon *that* which the ground bringeth forth, and upon men, and upon cattle, and

8. *The mountain, i.e.* the hill country; not Lebanon, from which they had received imports of cedar under the grant of Cyrus (cp. Ezra iii. 7). *I will take pleasure in it.* The people feared that the temple would be no credit to them: these promises assure them that it will not only be a credit to them, but a glory to God. The building will please Him and fully serve the purposes of a temple.

9. A resumption of ver. 6. *Ye looked for much, and, lo, it came to little.* The same idea is expressed by Isaiah (v. 10): "Ten acres of vineyard shall yield one bath [about six gallons of wine, not a gallon an acre], and the seed of an homer shall yield an ephah" [the ephah being the tenth part of an homer]. But even the pitiful crop that was brought home, *I did blow upon it;* which is commonly understood to mean, *I did scatter it as chaff,* but which may perhaps refer to the *blasting* effects of such a wind as is thus described by a traveller in Arabia: "In the month Marchesvan, a warm wind sometimes blew, which turned the ears yellow and they yielded no grain; it was an unsteady wind, but spoils all it touches" (cp. Isa. xl. 24). To the English reader the words convey the idea of contemptuous destruction, as if God had but to breathe in order to blight all their hopes, so dependent was their prosperity on Him (cp. to *pooh-pooh*). *Why? Because of mine house that is waste,* etc. The reason of all their failures and disappointments was that they had allowed God's house to remain in the ruinous, forsaken-looking state in which those who laid waste the city had left it. *Waste,* **destroyed, desolated, and rendered useless.** Cp. "waste wilderness," Deut. xxxii. 10, and Gower's lines:

"The field is where was the palais
The towne is *wast.*"

A building begun and abandoned, such as one may see at a street corner in bad times, is the very image of desolation. *Ye run every man unto his own house,* **ye display intense eagerness about your own homes.** To *run* is commonly used of the zealous pursuit of a purpose (cp. Isa. lix. 7; Jer. xxiii. 21).

10. *Is stayed,* better, hath kept back. *From dew,* **so that there is no dew.**

11. *I called,* as in 2 Kings viii. 1: "The Lord hath called for a famine, and it shall also come" (cp. Ps. cxlvii. 15). *Drought,* the Hebrew word is the same as that translated "waste" in ver. 9. Observe the Hebrew fondness for paronomasia, or playing upon words, and the idea of precise retribution which, as here, often underlies it. The word *drought* is not sufficiently general to apply to all the particulars enumerated in the verse, as *e.g.* "men."

12 upon all the labour of the hands. Then Zerubbabel the son of Shealtiel, and Joshua the son of Josedech, the high priest, with all the remnant of the people, obeyed the voice of the LORD their God, and the words of Haggai the prophet, as the LORD their God had sent him, and the people did fear
13 before the LORD. Then spake Haggai the LORD's messenger in the LORD's message unto the people, saying, I *am* with
14 you, saith the LORD. And the LORD stirred up the spirit of Zerubbabel the son of Shealtiel, governor of Judah, and the spirit of Joshua the son of Josedech, the high priest, and the spirit of all the remnant of the people; and they came and
15 did work in the house of the LORD of hosts, their God, In the four and twentieth day of the sixth month, in the second year of Darius the king.

[Drought is "that which drieth," and therefore the Scotch form of the word, drouth or drougth, is more correct. It was so written by Spenser and Bacon. It is used also by Robert Browning:

"In a sea-side house to the farther south
Where the baked cicalas die of *drouth*."]

12. *The remnant*, may be a simple equivalent for "**the rest**;" but the word is commonly used, as in Zech. viii. 6, of that small proportion of the people who returned from captivity, the remnant of the former flourishing population. *Obeyed*, lit. **hearkened unto.** They showed a disposition to obey, which Haggai met and encouraged by the assurance given in the 13th verse.

13. *I am with you*, not as a mere onlooker, not to stand by and see you fail, but to furnish you with Divine strength, to countenance you and give efficacy to your action. It is for your encouragement He says it. But were He to be with you and do nothing, that were no encouragement. He is with you because the work is His, because He has purposes to serve as well as you.

14. *Stirred up*, as if wakening one out of sleep (cp. Ezra i. 1, 5). There is apparently implied some direct action by God upon the mind of Zerubbabel and the rest.

15. *In the four and twentieth day*. Why the delay? The interval was probably spent in preparation. The foundation-stone seems to have been relaid in the 9th month (cp. ii. 10, 18).

What were the chief agricultural products of the land of Israel? What investments for his money were open to a Jew in these days? About what sum would the second temple cost? and the first?
Cite from the O. T. other instances of scarcity or famine following upon godlessness.
Cite instances, also from O. T., of good men suffering. What book of Scripture and what Psalms are written for the sake of solving this riddle?
Why were the Jews reprehensible for resolving in the first place to make themselves quite comfortable? Explain why and how we should put God first.

CHAPTER II.

1 IN the seventh *month*, in the one and twentieth *day* of the month, came the word of the LORD by the prophet Haggai,
2 saying, Speak now to Zerubbabel, the son of Shealtiel, governor of Judah, and to Joshua the son of Josedech, the
3 high priest, and to the residue of the people, saying, Who *is* left among you that saw this house in her first glory? and how do ye see it now? *is it* not in your eyes in comparison

SECOND PROPHECY (ii. 1–9).

Haggai encourages the people by assuring them that the temple they are building will have a glory greater than Solomon's.

1. *Seventh month*. Tisri, corresponding to part of September and October. The 21st day of this month was the seventh day of the feast of Tabernacles (cp. Lev. xxiii. 34). This was a festival, and the call to praise and thanksgiving in an unfinished and impoverished temple might naturally suggest gloomy and desponding thoughts. This state of mind was the moving cause of Haggai's message of encouragement.

3. The temple had been destroyed in the year 586 B.C. All who were upwards of seventy years old would therefore have some remembrance of it. And with the pardonable admiration of the institutions and ways of their youth which characterises old men, they were not slow to show their contempt for the new building (Ezra iii. 12). Their weeping was ill-timed, inconsiderate, and disheartening to the young. The confidence of youth is often blamed, but it is needed to bear up against the depreciation of the present which is dinned into their ears by those who can see no good in anything but that in which they were the chief actors. It is sad to be going back in the world, and to be put to shame by the very ruins left by our forefathers; but it is not always wise to express this sadness. *First glory.* The Jews were accustomed to say that five things were awanting in the second temple: 1. The sacred fire; 2. The Shekinah; 3. The ark and cherubim; 4. Urim and Thummim; 5. The spirit of prophecy (see Stanley, *Jewish Church*, ii. 203; and art. "Temple" in Smith's *Dict.*).

"If the measurements indicated in the decree of Cyrus were acted upon, the space which it covered and the height to which it rose were larger than the corresponding dimensions of its predecessor. It must have been in the absence of metal and carving that it was deemed so inferior to the first temple. The holy of holies was empty. The ark, the cherubs, the tables of stone, the vase of manna, the rod of Aaron were gone. The golden shields had vanished. Even the high priest, though he had recovered his official dress, had not been able to resume the breastplate with the oracular stones. Still there was not lacking a certain splendour and solidity befitting the sanctuary of a people once so great, and of a religion so self-contained" (Stanley, iii. 105).

Is it not in your eyes in comparison of it as nothing? better, Is not such an one [as this] as nothing in your eyes?

4 of it as nothing? Yet now be strong, O Zerubbabel, saith the LORD; and be strong, O Joshua, son of Josedech, the high priest; and be strong, all ye people of the land, saith the LORD, and work: for I *am* with you, saith the LORD of
5 hosts: *According to* the word that I covenanted with you when ye came out of Egypt, so my spirit remaineth among
6 you: fear ye not. For thus saith the LORD of hosts; Yet once, it *is* a little while, and I will shake the heavens, and
7 the earth, and the sea, and the dry *land;* And I will shake all nations, and the desire of all nations shall come: and I
8 will fill this house with glory, saith the LORD of hosts. The silver *is* mine, and the gold *is* mine, saith the LORD of hosts.

4. *Yet now be strong*, or, nerve yourself, pluck up your heart and persist, or, as Reuss translates (by the one French word), courage! The word is used of strengthening, making firm, and very significantly of hardening the heart in evil. Here it is a hardening of the heart in good that is enjoined.

5. *According to . . . so my spirit*, lit.: **The word which I covenanted with you when ye came out of Egypt, and my spirit.** The construction is broken, but the meaning is: The word which I covenanted with you remaineth—is still valid—and my Spirit remaineth among you. It was now a long time since the original covenant with the nation had been made (Ex. xix. and xxiv.), and the nation had passed through many phases and fortunes since that time; and these returned exiles might well be doubtful whether, after all that had come and gone, they could serve themselves heirs to the promises made to their forefathers. Hence this assurance. It is remarkable that the presence of the Spirit should be used as equivalent to a fulfilment of the covenant on God's part: the idea which pervades the N. T. (cp. Isa. lxiii. 10, 11, 14; and Neh. ix. 20).

6. *Yet once*, or once more, once again; as Sinai shook when the Lord descended to covenant with His people originally ("the whole mount quaked greatly," Ex. xix. 18; Ps. lxviii. 8; Hab. iii. 10), and as they were thus certified of His majesty and power as their God and King, so once again will He manifest His glory, and cause now all nations to tremble at His presence and acknowledge Israel's God (cp. Heb. xii. 18–29). This renewed manifestation of God's glory was to occur in a little while (see on ver. 9).

7. **The desire of all nations**, the desirable things of all nations, everything which the various nations count precious,—their wealth, glory, natural characteristics and special gifts and aptitudes,—shall be brought to beautify God's house (cp. Rev. xxi. 26). This meaning is determined by the words themselves and by ver. 8.

8. *The silver is mine.* The work I wish to do, I can command the means of doing. The silver and the gold at present held by those who are not thinking of this work, the money not as yet available for it, the means needful but of which there is at present no offer, promise, or sign—all this is mine. It is held by men on earth, some of them niggardly, some of them resolved on other investments, some of them hostile; it is held by men who look upon it as theirs, and who are destining it to uses of their own, but it is in reality mine, and will be used as I will.

9 The glory of this latter house shall be greater than of the former, saith the LORD of hosts: and in this place will I give peace, saith the LORD of hosts.

9. When the special glory and privilege of a generation passes away, there are many to lament its decay, but few to recognise the higher good that is taking its place. But God goes forward and not back, and is never so baffled as to be compelled to suspend progress. Let us not despise our own work nor our own generation. It also has a place in the history of God's work in the world.

In this place will I give peace. This is the sole and somewhat obscure intimation of the special and distinctive glory of the latter house (or, as it is better rendered, "**the latter glory of this house**"). To the contemporaries of Haggai his words undoubtedly conveyed the assurance that, amidst the threatened shaking of the nations, the people of God should be secure, undestroyed by surrounding convulsions. And, in point of fact, the house of God was preserved inviolate during the terrible conflict between the Persian and the Greek empires. This whole prediction of the latter glory of the temple was literally fulfilled, inasmuch as the means of building did not fail; but, as time wore on, and men became better able to understand what constituted the true glory of a dwelling-place of God, they must have seen that the tribute of the nations here predicted involved some more inward and spiritual recognition of God's house than mere pecuniary offerings. The Church often errs still in seeking a glory too external. It cannot compete with the world in what is distinctively the world's glory. Even Solomon's temple was far outdone by the golden house of Nero. The more spiritual men, therefore, would see in this prediction the assurance that the temple, as the visible centre of God's kingdom and place of His manifestation, was destined, notwithstanding its paltry appearance, to serve the purposes of God's dwelling on earth, and to command the attention and devotion of all men. And history unfolded the truth of these expectations (cp. Heb. xii. 26).

Note some of the resemblances and differences between the exodus and the return from Babylon. Specify those differences which might induce the fears alluded to in ver. 5 [e.g. the absence of miraculous interpositions].

Does ver. 5, or any passage of the O. T., suggest or involve the separate personality of the Holy Spirit?

The adoption of high-sounding ecclesiastical titles, the maintenance of brilliant and sensational services, the exercise of political influence—are these the proper glory of the Church, or do they exhibit her as a kind of second-rate world?

Apply to the Church of Christ and expand the idea contained in the words, " In this place will I give peace."

Comparing the last clause of i. 9 with ii. 4, state the proper value of energy; and criticise these lines:

> " And the sin I impute to each frustrate ghost
> Is the unlit lamp and the ungirt loin,
> Though the end in sight was a vice, I say."

10   In the four and twentieth *day* of the ninth *month*, in the second year of Darius, came the word of the LORD by Haggai
11   the prophet, saying, Thus saith the LORD of hosts; Ask now
12   the priests *concerning* the law, saying, If one bear holy flesh in the skirt of his garment, and with his skirt do touch bread, or pottage, or wine, or oil, or any meat, shall it be holy?
13   And the priests answered and said, No. Then said Haggai, If *one that is* unclean by a dead body touch any of these, shall it be unclean? And the priests answered and said, It
14   shall be unclean. Then answered Haggai, and said, So *is* this people, and so *is* this nation before me, saith the LORD; and so *is* every work of their hands; and that which they
15   offer there is unclean. And now, I pray you, consider from this day and upward, from before a stone was laid upon a

THIRD PROPHECY (ii. 10-19).

10. *In the four and twentieth day.* From ver. 18 we gather that on this day the actual rebuilding was begun; and this message is sent to remove an anxiety which might well dishearten the builders. Their past sacrifices seemed to have gone for nothing. Their harvests had still been bad: no blessing had come in acknowledgment of their prayers and offerings. If this was to continue, why rebuild the temple?
11. *Concerning the law*, or, **for instruction.**
12. See Lev. vi. 27, and Num. xix. 22. A holy thing does not communicate its holiness to whatever touches it, but, on the contrary, what is unclean contaminates what it touches. Put a decayed apple into a basket of sound fruit, it will not be turned into a fresh apple, but will communicate its rottenness.

" Will all great Neptune's ocean wash this blood
Clean from my hand? No; this my hand will rather
The multitudinous seas incarnadine,
Making the green one red."

Pottage, something prepared in a pot.
14. *So is this people.* The parable applies to the Jews, who, like the majority of Christians, had expected to be the better of sacrifices and services, irrespective of the evil of their selfish lives, and their neglect of the prime duty of building the temple. Haggai shows them that their good works had not compensated for their neglect, but that, on the contrary, their lack of zeal for God had vitiated all their religious services. Holy services do not cleanse unholy persons; unless there be a true repentance, the inward unrighteousness contaminates all (Ps. lxvi. 18; Prov. xxviii. 9).

Before me, **in my sight, in my judgment** (cp. Gen. vii. 1). The expression is also used of those who appear before God to sacrifice or intercede (cp. Jer. vii. 10, and xv. 1 (J. H. Michaelis).

15. *Upward, from before*, rather, **"backward, before."** Consider, he says, what has been your state until now; look back from this day when you are at last setting about this work in earnest. All the misery you have experienced in these days past has come of your neglect of this duty. Your

16 stone in the temple of the LORD: Since those *days* were, when *one* came to an heap of twenty *measures*, there were *but* ten: when *one* came to the pressfat for to draw out fifty *vessels*
17 out of the press, there were *but* twenty. I smote you with blasting and with mildew and with hail in all the labours of your hands; yet ye *turned* not to me, saith the LORD.
18 Consider now from this day and upward, from the four and twentieth day of the ninth *month*, *even* from the day that the
19 foundation of the LORD'S temple was laid, consider *it*. Is the seed yet in the barn? yea, as yet the vine, and the fig tree, and the pomegranate, and the olive tree, hath not brought forth: from this day will I bless *you*.

prayers for prosperity were unheard, because you remained impenitent about this matter.

16. *Twenty measures.* The precise quantity is not indicated. Henderson would understand **a heap of twenty sheaves.** It may quite as well denote a heap of threshed grain, the commonest grain measure being naturally understood; as when we speak of a man's age we say he is *forty* or *fifty* without expressing the easily-supplied *years.* The word denoting the measures drawn from the winefat (**vat**) is also indefinite.

18. *From this day and upward.* The expression being precisely the same as in the 15th verse, this also must be taken as a renewed exhortation to regard the *past*, to consider carefully what had been their condition down to, or, as he says, *up from* the very day on which he was speaking, the 24th of December. This day he apparently identifies with the day on which the foundation-stone of the temple was laid, although in chap. i. 15 he indicated that the building had been resumed three months before. And it is quite possible that the work which had so long been suspended would require three months of preparation, clearing away rubbish, testing exposed timber, renewing stores of material, and that when these three months were over some repetition of the ceremony of laying the foundation-stone might seem appropriate.

19. Haggai bids them observe that as yet no one could from any natural signs, from blossom or from any other natural augury, predict a good harvest. He does so that they might clearly understand that the coming prosperity was a response to their penitent zeal in reorganizing God's house. Had this prediction not been illustriously fulfilled, surely no one would have been hardy enough to publish it subsequent to its falsification.

From this day—not now from this day backwards, but **from this day onwards.** Down to this very hour all has been failure, but this day is a new point of departure.

> On *what ground was sacrifice accepted, if the mere offering of it was not pleasing to God? Explain the term* ex opere operato.
> Cp. Ex. xxi. 14 *with this passage, and show the difference between the law of sanctuary in Israel and in other countries.*
> Bacon says: "*Prosperity is the blessing of the O. T., adversity is the blessing of the New.*" *How far is this true?*
> "*A few days ago a man purchasing a fateereh of a baker in this city, saw him take out of his oven a dish of pork which he had been baking for a*

20 And again the word of the LORD came unto Haggai in the
21 four and twentieth *day* of the month, saying, Speak to Zerubbabel, governor of Judah, saying, I will shake the heavens
22 and the earth; And I will overthrow the throne of kingdoms, and I will destroy the strength of the kingdoms of the heathen; and I will overthrow the chariots, and those that ride in them; and the horses and their riders shall come
23 down, every one by the sword of his brother. In that day, saith the LORD of hosts, will I take thee, O Zerubbabel, my

> *Frank; and, supposing that the other things in the oven might have been in contact with the unclean meat, and thus contaminated, immediately brought a soldier from the nearest guard-house, and caused the baker to be conducted before the Zabit."* The case being too serious and difficult for the lower courts to determine, it was appealed to the *Muftee, who decided that all kinds of food not essentially impure were purified by contact with fire* (Lane's *Mod. Egyp.* i. 368).

FOURTH PROPHECY (ii. 20–23).

Assurance given that in approaching convulsions God's kingdom will stand.

20. The Jews might still have one cause of anxiety. Although assured that their religion would still exist, as it had existed even in Babylon, they might fear for their civil liberties. "It was to assure them that these fears were groundless that the prophet now comes forward. Hence he addresses Zerubbabel alone, and not Joshua, he being the civil leader, and therefore the representative of the people in their civil capacity. Some consider Zerubbabel here as a type of Christ, but this is only true in a secondary sense. The theocratic people were, in a certain sense, a type of Christ, and Zerubbabel was the representative of that people. To suppose it merely a prediction of the Messiah, under the name of Zerubbabel, would be greatly to narrow its significance, and cut off the link of consolation that was necessary to adapt it to the time when it was uttered. It involves Christ, but in a far wider sense than simply His person" (Moore). The continuity of God's kingdom—not merely of a principle or quality, but of an association of men from the beginning until now—amidst the decay of all other great empires is remarkable.

21. *I will shake the heavens.* Cp. ver. 6.

23. *A signet.* The ring engraved with the owner's name or device was used to impress a seal (Esther viii. 10), and became therefore the symbol of authority (see Gen. xli. 42; Esther iii. 10, and viii. 2). It was prized accordingly, and jealously guarded as a very precious object (see Jer. xxii. 24). In the British Museum may be seen the signet of King Thothmosis III., who probably lived B.C. 1320.

For I have chosen thee. This election by God is at the root of all the promised prosperity. Chosen for what? (cp. Ps. lxxviii. 70).

The Lord of Hosts: lit. Jehovah Tsevaoth. The reader will have noticed the frequency with which this title is used by Haggai. It occurs fourteen times in the two chapters. In Zechariah it occurs forty-eight times (according to Plumptre's reckoning), and twenty-five times in Malachi, while in the servant, the son of Shealtiel, saith the LORD, and will make thee as a signet: for I have chosen thee, saith the LORD of hosts.

Pentateuch it is not even once met with. The earliest mention of this name is in the prayer of Hannah (1 Sam. i. 3). It appears in the N. T. in one place only, and there in its untranslated form, Lord of *Sabaoth* (Jas. v. 4). (In Rom. ix. 29 it occurs in a quotation from the O. T.) The Hebrew word from which this title is formed is used both of the stars and of the angels, the visible objects in the material heavens, and the spiritual inhabitants of the invisible world; and the English word *host* is used as the equivalent of either of these meanings. Thus in Neh. ix. 6 we find the one word in both senses: "Thou, even Thou, art Jehovah alone; Thou hast made heaven, the heaven of heavens, with all their *host* . . . and the *host* of heaven worshippeth Thee" (cp. 1 Kings xxii. 19; Ps. ciii. 21; Luke ii. 13). The title, then, would seem to indicate Jehovah as Ruler and consequently Creator of the highest material objects and spiritual agencies. And it is supposed to have been chiefly used by the godly in Israel at times when the fascination of the worship of the heavenly bodies (Sabaism) was felt by the people. [Plato's idea of the stars as "divine and eternal animals" might be utilized to illustrate this subject. See the *Timæus*, c. 39.]

In what sense is this prophecy Messianic?
Collect passages illustrative of the meaning of the title "Lord of hosts." Shakespeare puts into the mouth of Henry V. the prayer, "O God of battles, steel my soldiers' hearts!"—is the title "Lord of hosts" ever connected in Scripture with armies of men, or only with the marshalled myriads of heaven?
Explain Jehovah, Adonai, El-Shaddai, Elohim.
Why do many modern scholars write the name Jehovah Yahveh, *and what is the history of the vowels in the word* "Jehovah"?

INTRODUCTION

TO

THE BOOK OF ZECHARIAH.

OF Zechariah's personal history almost nothing is known. He is introduced to us in this book as the son of Berechiah, and the grandson of Iddo. In Ezra v. 1 (also vi. 14) he is mentioned as "the son of Iddo;" and from this it has usually been concluded that his father Berechiah died while he was young, and that he was brought up as his grandfather Iddo's child. Some are disposed to find a confirmation of this in the circumstance that in the register of priests who returned from exile with Zerubbabel and Joshua, and which is given in Neh. xii., Zechariah is named as the successor of Iddo. If these persons are the prophet and his grandfather, as is by no means improbable, then, like Ezekiel and Jeremiah, Zechariah was a priest as well as a prophet.

The historical circumstances which show the relevancy of this prophet's utterances have already been indicated in the Introduction to the book of Haggai.

The book of Zechariah presents us with one of the nicest problems in the field of biblical criticism. Happily it is one, the solution of which has no bearing upon any point of dogmatic interest, and it may therefore be discussed impartially and without shrinking. Indeed, the difficulties in the way of our accepting all that is now contained in this book as the work of one and the same prophet were raised in the interests of a rigidly conservative orthodoxy. Mede, the great English writer on prophecy (who died in 1638), observing that the Evangelist Matthew (cp. xxvii. 9, 10) ascribes to Jeremiah a prediction which is nowhere found in the extant writings of that prophet, while it bears considerable resemblance to Zech. xi. 12, 13, concluded that the latter half of the book of Zechariah was not the work of the prophet who is described as the author of the first eight chapters. Of the latter chapters of the book he says: "Certainly, if a man weighs the contents of some of them, they should in all likelihood be of an older date than the time of Zachary—namely, before the captivity: for the subjects of some of them were scarce in being after that time. . . . There is no scripture saith they are Zachary's; but there is scripture saith that they are Jeremy's, as this of the Evangelist." Mede's argument, therefore, against the integrity of the book is twofold—the external evidence, furnished by Matthew's quotation, against the Zecharian authorship of the last chapters; and the internal evidence against this authorship furnished by these chapters themselves. The first of these arguments carries no weight. The argument from the internal evidence is, however, undoubtedly strong.

Every reader feels that in passing from the 8th to the 9th chapter of this book he is making a distinctly-marked transition to a new kind of writing. The first eight chapters are homogeneous, they have a resemblance to one another and obviously form one whole; but this continuity is broken by the remainder of the book. It is not only that the style changes, nor only that the interpreting angel who has figured so largely in the first part disappears from the second, in which his services are quite as much needed, but the subject and the character of the prophecies alter. In the first eight chapters the reference to Zechariah's own time is continual, pointed, and obvious; in the six remaining chapters there is no single allusion which obviously and without hesitation or dubiety can be referred to contemporary circumstances. In the former part of the book the prophet speaks of the half-built temple, of the gradually-extending city, of the measurers and masons, of the stones and the persons who were visible any day on the streets of Jerusalem, and which he had only to name to call up the real object before the mind's eye. Every one of his allusions could at once be understood by the men who were then resident at Jerusalem, and all his utterances regarded matters with which they themselves had to do. But no sooner do we read the first verse of the 9th chapter than we experience a sudden loss of this firm foothold among the well-known events of Zechariah's time. We seem to have made one step off *terra firma* into quaking bog, where we can walk only flounderingly. Up to the 9th chapter we advance in the clearest sunshine, we see standing out in broad day every person or thing that the prophet is aiming at; but in chap. ix. we walk into a bank of fog, we hear heavy firing,—very heavy firing indeed,—but we can only dimly and uncertainly make out the occasion and at whom the guns are directed.

This very marked difference between the first and second parts of the book has led many good men and good critics, first in our own and then in other countries, to conclude that these last chapters were anonymous, and were attached to the book of Zechariah for reasons now unknown—possibly because his book was the last of those whose authors were known by name, and fragments of unknown authorship were naturally appended there.

As a further reason for arriving at this conclusion, it has been urged that the nations spoken of in these closing chapters were in no way interesting to the Jews during the age of Zechariah. Now it is really of no great moment whether we refer the chapters in question to the time of Zechariah or to the time of Micah or Jeremiah. The point which is of interest is the principle used to determine the date of this or of any undated and anonymous prophecy. That principle is a very simple one: it is that the prophet is always sent in time of need to relieve present anxieties and to guide the people hopefully through emergencies which have already arisen. Prophecy, however high and far it soars in its flight when once begun, has always its starting-point from earth, from a spot within human eyesight and contemporary interest. It is not like a dream or portent which no one can interpret, and which has no apparent connection with any living interest. It does not introduce subjects with which the prophet's contemporaries are entirely unacquainted, nor does it predict events in which they are unconcerned. It is natural therefore to suppose that if a certain generation is assured that some neighbouring countries are to be laid waste, there is some practical interest of their own involved in this. If this country of ours were under a dispensation of prophecy, it is obvious that a prophet sent in the closing years of last century would have had nothing to say to our rulers about Afghanistan or Central Africa, but much to say of France, of Austria, and the other continental powers. And any prophet who could in our own day give no counsel about Eastern complications, but had much to say of the future of Peru or Norway, would simply be useless and prophesy without an audience.

If, then, it can be shown that it very deeply concerned some particular generation of Israel to be made aware of a coming event, and that the knowledge of this event did not at all concern any other generation, this will of itself afford very strong presumption that the prophecy which predicts the event in question dates from the generation which behoved to know it.

Applying this criterion to the 9th chapter, it would appear that the reason why Zechariah's generation is made aware of the approaching calamities which were to fall on neighbouring peoples is disclosed in the 8th verse. God's house was being rebuilt by that generation; they were spending large sums of money upon it, and for its sake were provoking the envy and hostility of their neighbours, and it could scarcely fail to occur to them that very likely all this would be in vain. They were a small and weak people, and could not expect to cope with such empires as had previously laid their temple in ruins, or with that new Greek power which was already strangling serpents in its cradle. Nothing could be more appropriate than to give to this generation those very encouragements and assurances which fill this 9th chapter. It is a translation into actual circumstances of the words, "A thousand shall fall at thy side, and ten thousand at thy right hand; but it shall not come nigh thee." The impregnable stronghold of Tyre was to be taken; the proud, unconquered, fierce Philistines were to sink before some fiercer, more unconquerable invader; how then should the weaklings who feared a few Samaritans stand before such an enemy? "I will encamp about mine house because of the army." The King of Israel would come and do battle for them, not with the war-chariot and battle bow, but with meekness and peace. I will raise up "thy sons, O Zion, against thy sons, O Greece," and make thee "as the sword of a mighty man."

It is true, this explicit reference to Greece has the appearance of being premature, even in Zechariah's time. As a rule, "prophets threaten no people, and promise nothing of any, till the people itself is come on the scene and into relation with their people." And although Greece was considerably before the attention of the Jews during the reign of Cyrus, they had not since his death been in a position very seriously to threaten any dependency of Persia. It was only after the battle of Marathon (B.C. 490) that the Greeks fairly entered the political horizon as a power likely to prove itself formidable to its eastern neighbours. And it is, of course, possible that this prophecy may have been uttered or penned even by Zechariah subsequently to that date. The Jews may have taken alarm as soon as they saw the tide turning against their Persian protectors. They may have taken alarm all the more readily, because the fleets which had been chiefly instrumental in chastising and reducing the rebellious Ionians were Phœnician fleets, and the vengeance of Greece would certainly fall heavily on these sea-going populations which lived in dangerous proximity to Israel.

It may be questioned, however, whether it is not more likely that the fears which this prophecy was intended to allay were general, and created by the conscious inferiority of the Jews, and were not due to any specific and obvious danger. In quieting this fear the prophet uses language which is not general, but specific, and takes occasion from the undefined alarm to promise a definite deliverance. For it seems obvious that the deliverance sketched in this chapter is that which was wrought nearly 200 years after when Alexander took Tyre, and marched south upon the Philistines, but spared Jerusalem. "No explanation of the whole section (ix. 1-x. 17) is possible, if it be not gained from the history of Alexander the Great. History relates expressly how, after the battle of Issus, he took possession of all Syria and Zidon without much difficulty; how, with an employment of military contrivance unheard of elsewhere, he conquered and destroyed island Tyre; how, of the maritime cities of Philistia, with indomitable perseverance he besieged and took Gaza, and punished with death the opposition of its commander." These are the words of a very free-thinking but unusually clear-headed critic. At the same time, if we put Greece out of account, there can be no question that the other countries and cities named in chap. ix. were very much before the mind of the Hebrews at a much earlier period of their history. Hanun, king of Gaza, was taken prisoner by Sargon. Sennacherib subdued the king of Ashdod. The king of Ashkelon was dethroned, and a vassal of Assyria put in his place. The princes of Ekron were slain and impaled. Hadrach (or Syria) was subdued and annexed to Assyria as early as the reign of Ahaz. Hamath was conquered about the same period. And a comparison of this ninth chapter with the first chapter of Amos does make one hesitate to affirm that two prophecies so similar could be uttered at periods so widely apart as the close of the ninth century and the beginning of the fifth. But so difficult is it to account for the allusion to Greece at the earlier period, and so peculiar to Zechariah are one or two expressions used (ver. 8), and so appropriate is the promise of the eighth verse to the age of the temple restoration, that the evidence of the ninth chapter would seem, on the whole, to be in favour of the later date.

In chap. x. we meet with other allusions which at first sight seem to correspond rather with the earlier than with the post-exile date. Egypt and Assyria are spoken of as if they were the nations which at that time were specially formidable to Judah and Israel (chap. x. 8 to end). But after the captivity, in the time of Zechariah, the days of Assyrian greatness were past, and Egypt was not in any threatening attitude. "The only other prophets to whom these two nations appear as formidable, *at the same time,* are Hosea (vii. 11, xii. 1) and Isaiah (vii. 18) ; and that in prophecies which must have been uttered between 743 and 740." But even these, and other historical circumstances alluded to by the prophet, although at first sight they seem very strongly to favour the hypothesis of an earlier date, cannot be said utterly to preclude the idea of the Zecharian authorship. For although Assyria was now merely a part of the Persian empire, it was yet that part of it which had the most important connection with Judah, and was so prominent to the Jew that he called the Persian emperor the "King of Assyria" (see Ezra vi. 22). And as regards Egypt, not only had captive Jews been deported into Egypt, but the relation of Egypt as an unwilling vassal to Persia made the position of Judah precarious in the extreme during the lifetime of Zechariah. Besides, it is difficult, if not impossible, to reconcile the expressions of the sixth verse with a date long anterior to the exile. Naturally these expressions are accepted as implying that already the people had been "cast off."

Another serious difficulty in the way of accepting the latter portion of the book as of post-exilian origin is the following. In chap. xi. a symbolic representation is given which is intended to portray a threatened disruption of Judah and Israel. "I cut asunder mine other staff, even bands, that I might break the brotherhood between Judah and Israel." This threat would seem to imply that as yet that brotherhood was unbroken. The prophecy would have been meaningless had it been spoken during the period when already Judah and Israel were existing in alienation, if not hostility, as separate kingdoms. We must refer it therefore either to the time previous to the secession of the ten tribes under Jeroboam, or to the time subsequent to the captivity when the hostility had died out. We can have little hesitation in deciding between these two periods. After the captivity Judah and Israel (so far as Israel existed at all) existed as one united people; but the threat of dismemberment and scattering is conveyed in the old terms which had once been filled with so real a significance. A disintegration was to go on in the nation which would, in point of fact, be very different from, and even more fatal than, the rupture of the tribes, but which could best be predicted in the old, well-understood language. It was after the price of the Good Shepherd had been weighed that the bond binding the Jews together as a nation was burst.

It has recently been alleged by one whose opinion on such a point is most worthy of consideration (T. K. Cheyne), that the manner in which the mourning for Josiah is mentioned in chap. xii. 11 shows that this catastrophe was still fresh in remembrance, and had not yet been cast into the shade by the still more overwhelming sorrow of the destruction of Jerusalem—in other words, that the author of this passage was a contemporary of Jeremiah. This is doubtful. In chap. xiv. a much more remote event, the earthquake in the days of Uzziah, is still used as a typical instance of such calamities. And, besides, the death of a favourite king, slain in battle for his people, will never pass out of the national remembrance, nor will the national mourning caused by that event cease to be used by a poet as the type of a people's lamentations for their champion who has died for them.

Indeed, this very passage would seem to present one of the strongest arguments in favour of the post-exilian date,[1] inasmuch as the sufferings of the Messiah are more distinctly alluded to than was possible at an earlier period. The aspect of the Messiah as a sufferer was certainly of late development; as was also that identification of the Messiah or of God's messenger with Jehovah Himself, which is one of the most marked characteristics both of the former and of the latter parts of this book (cp. the interchange of "me" and "him" in chap. xii. 10, and the interchange of "sender" and "sent" in xi. 13 and ii. 11). We do not mean to say that such a passage as xii. 10 could not have been penned before the exile, but only that between the former and the latter part of the book there is an agreement in the general idea of the relation of the Messiah to Jehovah, and that this idea is certainly of late development.

The last difficulty in the way of accepting the integrity of this book is that according to chap. xiii. 2 it would seem as if idolatry still held its ground in the land of Judah, and as if there still existed many false prophets and diviners. But these were the scandals and abuses rather of the age of Jeremiah and Ezekiel than of the purer post-exile period during which idolatry was unknown. This, however, is somewhat too sweeping an assertion, for it is certain that Nehemiah strove against mixed marriages chiefly because they seduced to idolatry, and brought the children under heathen

[1] In favour of the post-exilian date the prominence given to the feast of Tabernacles might be pleaded, and possibly also the "bells of the horses."

influences. And Malachi (iii. 5) had still to protest against the sorcerers.

After carefully weighing all that is alleged on either side, and studying the book itself with the closest attention, many will probably agree with Canon Perowne that "it is not easy to say which way the weight of evidence preponderates." That which in some minds gives a preponderating weight to the evidence in favour of the integrity of the book, is the fact (which any one can verify for himself with the aid of a well-stored memory or a reference Bible) that the author of the second half of the book shows familiarity with the writings of Ezekiel and the pre-exile prophets. It is barely possible that they may have borrowed from him, much more probable that he borrowed from them.

Among the critics who deny the integrity of the book, there is great diversity of opinion (see Pusey's tabulated view) regarding the date of the second part. Bleek, as being one of the most exact and conservative of this class, may be cited: "I am decidedly of opinion that (1) the prophecies of this second part, as a whole, are not to be ascribed to the prophet Zechariah, who lived after the captivity, but that they were composed at an earlier time, and before the captivity; and (2) that chap. ix.–xi. belong to an earlier time than chap. xii.–xiv., —the former to the age of the very earliest prophets whose writings have been preserved to us, viz. to the age of Uzziah and Ahaz; the latter to the age of Jeremiah,—and therefore that these two sections must have been written by different prophets." In this view there is nothing intrinsically objectionable; but if it is true, then it would seem as if verses 6–9 of chap. xiii. must have fallen out of their place at the close of chap. xi. Besides, there are coincidences of expression between the two proposed divisions which seem to indicate that they are from one hand (cp. x. 6, last clause, with xiii. 9).

ZECHARIAH.

CHAPTER I.

1 IN the eighth month, in the second year of Darius, came the word of the LORD unto Zechariah, the son of Berechiah,
2 the son of Iddo the prophet, saying, The LORD hath been
3 sore displeased with your fathers. Therefore say thou unto them, Thus saith the LORD of hosts; Turn ye unto me, saith the LORD of hosts, and I will turn unto you, saith the LORD
4 of hosts. Be ye not as your fathers, unto whom the former prophets have cried, saying, Thus saith the LORD of hosts;

INTRODUCTORY SUMMONS TO REPENTANCE (i. 1–6).

1. *Eighth month*, the month most nearly corresponding to our November, and which before the exile was called **Bul**, and afterwards **Marchesvan**, a name supposed to be derived from the constant dripping rain which characterised the month (but cp. Ezra x. 9). This first recorded prophecy of Zechariah overlaps the work of Haggai, being two months after his first prophecy, a week or two after his second, and a month before his third. This summons to repentance is appropriate even after the promises made by Haggai, because these were conditional on repentance.

Iddo the prophet, should be **Iddo, the prophet**, the designation referring to Zechariah, not to Iddo.

2. *The Lord hath been sore displeased*: lit. **hath been angry with anger**. The word seems originally to mean **breaking out in long-controlled indignation**. *Sore* (cp. German *schwer*, *sehr*) used as an intensive, and not here represented by any separate word in the original.

3. *Unto them*—that is, not the fathers, but those to whom the prophet was to be sent, and about whom he is represented as receiving instructions. Observe the threefold repetition of the emphatic "*saith the Lord of hosts*," giving prominence to the authority of the message, as if God were swearing by Himself.

Turn ye unto me. "When it is said in Scripture, 'Turn ye unto me and I will turn unto you,' we are reminded of our free will. When we reply, 'Turn us to Thee, O Lord, and we shall be turned,' we confess that we are first aided [*præveniri*] by the grace of God" (*Concil. Trident.* vi. 5, cited by Pusey).

4. *Be ye not as your fathers.* Do not turn away as they did from the voice of the prophets summoning them to repentance. If they were not to

Turn ye now from your evil ways, and *from* your evil doings:
but they did not hear, nor hearken unto me, saith the LORD.
5 Your fathers, where *are* they? and the prophets, do they live
6 for ever? But my words and my statutes, which I commanded my servants the prophets, did they not take hold of
your fathers? and they returned and said, Like as the LORD
of hosts thought to do unto us, according to our ways, and
according to our doings, so hath he dealt with us.

have their fathers' experience, they must have more than their fathers'
godliness.

5, 6. *Your fathers . . . dealt with us.* These words are intended to meet
the thought which naturally arose in the mind of those who were restored to
their own country, that they were a new people without the same ominous
threats hanging over them as their fathers had incurred. Zechariah reminds
them that their fathers' fate is the best prophet to them. ("Aujourd'hui,
l'avertissement le plus éloquent et le plus pressant, c'est l' histoire," Reuss.)
Your fathers and the prophets are alike gone, but the testimony your fathers
bore to the truth of the prophets' warnings remains. You have not the same
warnings ringing in your ears that your fathers had, you have not men like
Jeremiah to move you to godliness, the prophets do not live for ever; but you
have what your fathers had not, you have the awful truthfulness of God's
words of warning written in your fathers' fate.

Take hold of, rather, **overtake,** as of a dogged pursuer. (Illustrate from
Plutarch's *Delays in Divine Justice;* Æschylus, *Eumenides;* Horace, *Carm.*
iii. 2, 31: "Rarely has punishment, though lame, failed to overtake the
criminal fleeing before her.")

> *Give an account of the conquest and captivity of Israel and Judah.*
> *What prophets were chiefly occupied with warning the people of the coming*
>   *captivity?*
> *Give other instances of God's threatenings being fulfilled.*
> *Can you give any instances of people learning by the experience of others?*
> *Give passages which contain the idea of punishment dogging a person;*
>   *and explain the fable that represents the dying eagle as recognising*
>   *that the arrow that had pierced him was feathered from his own wing.*

FIRST VISION: THE HORSEMAN AMONG THE MYRTLES (i. 7–17).

It was now four months since Haggai had assured the people that in "a
little while" God would "shake the kingdoms," and out of this shaking
bring increased glory to their temple and state. They were now growing
impatient at the delay. One Persian mail after another came in, one and
another caravan toiled up the steep ascent to Jerusalem and was eagerly met
by the inhabitants, but yet no word of the "shaking." They were beginning
to question whether the promise of God was meant to have any practical
fulfilment. To meet this rising impatience and unbelief the following vision
is sent. And the substantial meaning of it is, that to every one who has an
eye for spiritual realities, the angel of the Lord [*i.e.* God Incarnate] appears,

7 Upon the four and twentieth day of the eleventh month, which *is* the month Sebat, in the second year of Darius, came the word of the LORD unto Zechariah, the son of Berechiah,
8 the son of Iddo the prophet, saying, I saw by night, and behold a man riding upon a red horse, and he stood among the myrtle trees that *were* in the bottom; and behind him
9 *were there* red horses, speckled, and white. Then said I, O my lord, what *are* these? And the angel that talked with
10 me said unto me, I will show thee what these *be*. And the man that stood among the myrtle trees answered and said, These *are they* whom the LORD hath sent to walk to and fro
11 through the earth. And they answered the angel of the LORD that stood among the myrtle trees, and said, We have walked

keeping watch for His people; Himself sitting ready mounted to interfere in their behalf, and His swift couriers incessantly pouring in from all parts of the earth. Assurance is given that the most alert intelligence is charged with the interests of God's people, and that He who rules them is kept advised of each minutest circumstance that can affect them.

7. *Sebat*, corresponding most nearly to **February**. *Came the word*, a general expression for any kind of revelation; this was by vision.

8. *A man riding*, called in ver. 11 "**the angel of the Lord.**"
Bottom, cp. *As you like it*, iv. 3, 77, **a plot of low-lying ground, a shady place.** It was probably an actual spot well known to the prophet, and to which he was possibly accustomed to retire for prayer and solitude, as our Lord to the olive orchard outside Jerusalem. Often in this quiet spot he had himself used the words of the 12th verse. This had been the burden of his thoughts as he nervously paced under the shadow of the myrtles, this his uniform cry as he cast himself pained and perplexed on the earth beneath them. But familiar as was the myrtle grove, it was to-night thronged with figures before unseen. The mounted scouts of Jehovah seemed to be gathering from all parts of the earth to give in their reports. The interpreting angel finds no significance in the various colours; we may suppose therefore that their chief purpose was to distinguish the horses as coming from different countries.

9. *O my lord*, probably addressed to the angel that talked with him, though as yet he has not been mentioned.

11. The reports presented an unusual agreement. The earth in every part seemed to be enjoying a time of peace and rest. God's people alone are in trouble. It is to the **angel of Jehovah** these reports are given in. This is the term appropriated to the angel who represents Jehovah as distinguished from angels sent upon special commissions to do some particular occasional service. The angel of the Lord speaks and acts as Jehovah, so that in Ex. iii., after the writer has said "the angel of Jehovah appeared" (ver. 2), he goes on to say (ver. 4), in reference to the same person, "When Jehovah saw." Whether this angel of Jehovah has a separate individual existence of his own, or is merely a passing mode of Jehovah's self-manifestation, it is difficult to say. "The *function* of the angel so entirely overshadows his *personality*, that the O. T. does **not ask who or what** this angel **is, but what he does.** And the answer to this

to and fro through the earth, and, behold, all the earth sitteth
12 still, and is at rest. Then the angel of the LORD answered
and said, O LORD of hosts, how long wilt thou not have mercy
on Jerusalem and on the cities of Judah, against which thou
13 hast had indignation these threescore and ten years? And
the LORD answered the angel that talked with me *with* good
14 words *and* comfortable words. So the angel that communed
with me said unto me, Cry thou, saying, Thus saith the LORD
of hosts; I am jealous for Jerusalem and for Zion with a
15 great jealousy. And I am very sore displeased with the
heathen *that are* at ease: for I was but a little displeased,
16 and they helped forward the affliction. Therefore thus saith
the LORD; I am returned to Jerusalem with mercies: my
house shall be built in it, saith the LORD of hosts, and a line
17 shall be stretched forth upon Jerusalem. Cry yet, saying,
Thus saith the LORD of hosts; My cities through prosperity
shall yet be spread abroad; and the LORD shall yet comfort
Zion, and shall yet choose Jerusalem.

question is, that he represents God to man so directly and fully, that when he speaks or acts God Himself is felt to speak or act" (Robertson Smith).

12. The contrast between the prosperous condition of all other nations and the depressed state of Israel provokes the man on the red horse to cry out: How is it that the one dark spot in a bright and joyful earth is precisely that spot where God's people dwell? Or it may be that these scouts had been sent out to see if there were any signs of that shaking of the nations which was to be Israel's deliverance. But there are no signs, and hence the passionate entreaty of ver. 12. The *threescore and ten years* are calculated from the destruction of Jerusalem in 588 B.C.

13. The good and comfortable words, though not directly reported, no doubt substantially reappear in the succeeding verses.

14. So little is outward condition the index of our relation to God, that He was displeased with the heathen who were reported as everywhere at ease, while He was burning to avenge His people, and raise them out of their ignoble condition.

15. *Helped forward.* The Chaldeans had overstepped their commission, and inflicted a harsher punishment than God saw to be needful.

16. *A line.* The measuring line of the builders who are to restore the city.

17. *My cities through prosperity shall yet be spread abroad*, rather, **shall again overflow with prosperity** (cp. ver. 12 and chap. ii.).

Explain the symbolism of colours in Scripture and in our own country (cp. Rev. vi. 5, etc.).
Mention passages in the O. and N. T. in which the Persian postal system is referred to. (*Posts*, etymologically, *mounted couriers posted*, positi, *on the leading roads of the empire, ready to carry forward a message.*)
Collect passages illustrating the function of the Angel of Jehovah.

18 Then lifted I up mine eyes, and saw, and behold four horns.
19 And I said unto the angel that talked with me, What *be* these?
And he answered me, These *are* the horns which have scattered
20 Judah, Israel, and Jerusalem. And the LORD showed me
21 four carpenters. Then said I, What come these to do?
And he spake, saying, These *are* the horns which have
scattered Judah, so that no man did lift up his head: but
these are come to fray them, to cast out the horns of the
Gentiles, which lifted up *their* horn over the land of Judah to
scatter it.

Hadas *is the Hebrew for* a myrtle: *what feminine name was derived from it?*
Practical. *While we look at what is visible to the bodily eye, we may fancy we are left to bear our burden alone; but when the veil is lifted, we see that there is a heart above, moved by our sorrow and weighted with thought for our deliverance. While we are thinking that our efforts to set matters right are either unobserved or discountenanced by any higher power, there is really a grave and full consideration, a majestic and moving intercession proceeding in our behalf, an activity to which ours is as negligence, a sense of responsibility which accepts and discharges the duties attaching to the management of all human interests.*

SECOND VISION: THE FOUR HORNS AND FOUR CARPENTERS (chap. i. 18–21).

This vision follows in natural sequence upon the first, and should therefore not be separated from it by being set in a new chapter as it is in the Hebrew Bible. It gives assurance that the distresses of God's people are now to be ended. The horns which had tossed and gored Israel are to be prevented from doing further injury.

18. *Horns* were shown to the prophet as the symbol of power, especially of military power (cp. 1 Kings xxii. 11; Micah iv. 13; Dan. viii. 20, 21). *Four* horns were seen, as representing the totality of Israel's enemies—her enemies from all quarters. It cannot indicate four distinct powers, neither more nor less.

19. *What be these?*—i.e. **What are these?** Here the antiquated use of "be" can do no harm; but in Judg. xvi. 9 it misleads, making that appear to be a wish or a summons which is only an announcement of fact (cp. *Bible Word-Book*). *Israel* is mentioned as well as Judah; one of the indications that the old discord had been forgotten in their common calamity.

20. *Carpenters*, craftsmen, workmen, men of skill and strength (cp. Ezek. xxi. 31, where this word is rendered *skilful*, to destroy).

21. *So that no man did lift up his head,* resistance was out of the question. Helpless despair was the result of this furious butting and tossing. The captivity crushed and humbled. *Fray* does not mean to rub or file down, as the English reader might suppose, but to *terrify* (cp. Deut. xxviii. 26). It is the root of the verb *affray*, of which *afraid* (affrayed) is the participle (*Bible Word-Book*). The expression has a reference to the secure case of the nations, ver. 15.

> Explain the symbolic use of "*horns.*" *Why was the horn used as the symbol of plenty in the cornucopiæ? Its use as an article of dress is illustrated in Van Lennep's* Bible Lands, *p.* 528. (*The same symbolism was in use among the Romans; cp. Horace,* Carm. ii. 19, 29, iii. 21, 18.)
> *What would probably give men the idea of* four *directions?*
> *Is punishment always removed as soon as there is a hearty submission to God?* (*Observe the indignation of God against what injures His people: how He endures what afflicts us only as a temporary expedient to work in us a capacity for greater good.*)
> *Who were the "workmen" who in fact "frayed the horns of the Gentiles"?*

CHAPTER II.

1 I LIFTED up mine eyes again, and looked, and behold a
2 man with a measuring line in his hand. Then said I, Whither goest thou? And he said unto me, To measure Jerusalem, to see what *is* the breadth thereof, and what *is*
3 the length thereof. And, behold, the angel that talked with me went forth, and another angel went out to meet him,
4 And said unto him, Run, speak to this young man, saying,

THIRD VISION: THE SURVEYOR FORBIDDEN TO MEASURE JERUSALEM (ii. 1–13).

The object of this vision was to encourage the present inhabitants of Jerusalem to expect a large increase to the population, and consequently to the size of their city.

1. *I lifted up mine eyes again, and looked, and behold,* a repetition of the formula translated in chap. i. 18, **Then lifted I up mine eyes, and saw, and behold** *a man with a measuring line,* in fulfilment of i. 16. The vision of Zechariah was based on what was in his thoughts and under his eye from day to day—plans for restoring the city. He saw a man proceeding to take measurements for the laying out of the streets and walls, to see what the present size and capabilities of the city were, and what might be made of the ruins (cp. Ezek. xl. and Rev. xi. 1 and xxi. 15, 16).

3. *The angel that talked with me* is the interpreting angel who has figured in the two preceding visions: another angel goes out to meet this angel.

4. The *young man* is the man with the measuring line. The angel is directed to *run* to meet him, that he may prevent him from carrying out his purpose of measuring the city. He is to show him that his purpose of marking out boundaries and walls is useless, because the city is destined to

Jerusalem shall be inhabited *as* towns without walls for the
5 multitude of men and cattle therein: For I, saith the LORD,
will be unto her a wall of fire round about, and will be the
6 glory in the midst of her. Ho, ho, *come forth*, and flee from
the land of the north, saith the LORD: for I have spread you
abroad as the four winds of the heaven, saith the LORD.
7 Deliver thyself, O Zion, that dwellest *with* the daughter of
8 Babylon. For thus saith the LORD of hosts; After the glory
hath he sent me unto the nations which spoiled you: for he
9 that toucheth you toucheth the apple of his eye. For,
behold, I will shake mine hand upon them, and they shall
be a spoil to their servants: and ye shall know that the

exceed all ordinary dimensions, and become so great that no walls will be capable of containing it. It will overflow into suburbs, adjoining villages, and even annex the neighbouring towns, so as to present the appearance not of a walled city, but of a densely-peopled district. "*Jerusalem shall be inhabited as towns without walls,*" or, **as open country**, denotes also that security as well as magnitude will characterize the future city.

5. No danger will attend the extra-mural overflow predicted in ver. 4, for as in old times Jerusalem gloried in the strength of her natural position and seemingly impregnable fortifications, so now "*I will be unto her a wall of fire round about*" (cp. 1 Sam. xxv. 16: "They were a wall unto us all the while we were keeping the sheep"). The expression "a wall of fire" was probably first suggested in the wilderness days by the camp fires which outlying parties used to scare the wild beasts.

6. **Ho, ho, flee ye then from the land of the north.** God summons those of His people who remained in Babylon to return to their own land, and that quickly, for there was but a year or two to spare before Darius sacked that city. The reason of this summons might have been gathered from the preceding promise of prosperity to Jerusalem, but is repeated in the words of this verse, which should *probably* be translated "**for I will spread you abroad as the four winds of heaven**," *i.e.* in all directions you will expand.

7. *Deliver thyself, O Zion.* It is better to retain the exclamation of the original, and translate literally: **Ho, Zion, deliver thyself, thou that dwellest as a daughter of Babylon.**

8. *After the glory:* lit. after glory, to win glory, in the manner described in ver. 9, by bringing manifest divine judgment on the spoilers of Israel. Who is the "me" that speaks of himself as "sent"? As there has been no break in the utterance of the angel who went out to speak to the interpreting angel, it would seem as if this angel speaks still. And as no care is taken to distinguish this angel from the Lord of hosts, but, on the contrary, in ver. 11 he speaks as if he were himself Jehovah, we must conclude that the speaker is the angel of the Lord. *Apple of his eye:* lit. **the aperture, the gate of the eye.** [But the Hebrew word *baba* may be equivalent to the word used in Deut. xxxii. 10, which means "little man," and to our own "*pupil*" = little boy.]

9. In the fourth or fifth year of Darius, the Babylonians, after long and cautious plotting, revolted and shut themselves up in their city, prepared for a

10 LORD of hosts hath sent me. Sing and rejoice, O daughter of Zion: for, lo, I come, and I will dwell in the midst of
11 thee, saith the LORD. And many nations shall be joined to the LORD in that day, and shall be my people: and I will dwell in the midst of thee, and thou shalt know that the
12 LORD of hosts hath sent me unto thee. And the LORD shall inherit Judah his portion in the holy land, and shall choose
13 Jerusalem again. Be silent, O all flesh, before the LORD: for he is raised up out of his holy habitation.

long siege. Zopyrus, Darius' friend and general, cut off his own ears and nose, and by pretending that he had been thus mutilated by Darius, gained entrance into the city and the confidence of the besieged. By his craft the gates were opened to the Persians, and when the city was mastered 3000 Babylonian nobles were crucified.

10, 11. Cp. ver. 5. God came and dwelt in the midst of His people when the temple of Zerubbabel was set apart for His worship; but the promise, "*many nations shall be joined to the Lord in that day*," was not fulfilled until God dwelt with men in the human body of Jesus, which the temple had foreshadowed. [On the interchange of persons in this verse, cp. ver. 8.]

12. *Judah his portion.* Cp. Deut. xxxii. 9; 1 Sam. x. 1; Ps. lxxviii. 71. *In the holy land,* holy because God inhabits it in a special manner. Cp. Ex. xv. 13 and 17. Cp. also the expressions "the holy city," "my holy mountain," etc. The word *choose* is used in a sense pregnant with all the issues and results of God's choosing a people as His peculiar people (cp. i. 17).

13. *Be silent:* lit. Hush (Hebrew *Has* = st.). Cp. Hab. ii. 20. *His holy habitation, i.e.* the unseen heaven. God is said to rise up out of His habitation when He manifests His presence by striking judgments or mercies. The word *habitation* denotes an inaccessible dwelling. It is used of the den, lair, covert of a wild beast, or of any place of retreat, refuge, or defence.

REMARKS.—1. The restored inhabitants of Jerusalem were liable to make the mistake so often made by municipal corporations of making no provision for the future. The original city walls close to the heart of the town, the cramped streets, the inadequate water supply, the meagre provision both for dead and living, all remind us how prone people are to forget that well-placed cities grow. The church runs the same danger, and must beware of running up walls which can only cramp her and retard her expansion. She is destined to be world-wide, but she makes herself local in so far as she identifies herself with practices which it is impossible for some men to adopt, or with forms of thought which suit only half the world, or with traditions which have grown up of late years. Sound creeds, reasonable forms of worship, wholesome practices, are all very useful, but they are not the best defence of the Church, and may be the means of limiting and retarding her growth. Naturally, we fear we shall be trodden out by the world if we have not a well-defined and solid wall around us, through the gates of which none can pass without scrutiny. But, in point of fact, it is not the external wall, but the spirit within, which is the defence; it is only the inhabitation of God which can preserve the Church.

2. This increase of population was to arise partly from the return of more of the Jews from Babylon (ver. 7). But they required a very loud summons. They had become rooted in the land of captivity. As the child who is banished to another room is at first wild with misery, but speedily finds amusement and is sorry to be recalled: as the Christian who feels at first distressed by the low spiritual condition into which he has fallen by his sin, but gradually becomes used to it, forgets his spiritual joys and finds pleasure in the world; so was it with the exiled Jews.

3. They who would not obey this summons would share in the overthrow of Babylon. The troops of Darius would make no nice distinctions between Jew and Babylonian. And the ordinary visitations and disasters that wait upon wrong-doing make no nice distinctions between those who profess themselves of the world and those who assume to be something better. Commercial distress makes no distinction between the man who has overdriven his business on avowedly worldly principles, and the man who has overspeculated, while he has also nursed himself in the belief that he is a child of God. A child of God he may be, but if this has not prevented him from behaving like a man of the world, it will not prevent him suffering as men of the world suffer. Natural law is no respecter of persons. Justice is blind, and weighs deeds irrespective of the person who has thrown them into her scale.

Illustrate from Scripture the expressions "he that toucheth you toucheth the apple of his eye;" "I will dwell in the midst of thee" (cp. tabernacle, tent, etc.); and "the Lord shall inherit Judah, His portion."

Compare with ver. 5, "Britannia needs no bulwarks," and Bacon's saying: "Walled towns, stored arsenals and armouries, goodly races of horse, chariots of war, elephants, ordnance, artillery, and the like; all this is but a sheep in a lion's skin, except the breed and disposition of the people be stout and warlike."

Account for Nehemiah's conduct in fortifying Jerusalem although this prophecy had been uttered. And compare with this prophecy of teeming population, Neh. vii. 4 and xi. 1.

CHAPTER III.

1 AND he shewed me Joshua the high priest standing before the angel of the LORD, and Satan standing at his right hand

FOURTH VISION: JOSHUA THE HIGH PRIEST ACCEPTED AND BLESSED AS THE PEOPLE'S REPRESENTATIVE (iii. 1-10).

Object of the Vision.—To restore the people's confidence in the priesthood and their ministry. In commencing to rebuild the temple, the people naturally felt some doubt whether it was any use doing so. A temple without an inhabiting God is a mockery, and they had so much doubt about

2 to resist him. And the LORD said unto Satan, The LORD
rebuke thee, O Satan; even the LORD that hath chosen
Jerusalem rebuke thee: *is* not this a brand plucked out of

the return of God to their midst as made them welcome the promise of the preceding vision: "I will dwell in the midst of thee." But they needed a further assurance. They felt that they had sinned, and that their priests had sinned with them. They felt the justice of Ezekiel's words (xxii. 26): "Her priests have violated my law, and have profaned mine holy things," and they were not sure how the services of these priests would now be received by their holy God. The vision therefore takes its starting-point from this feeling which prevailed among the people. Joshua is seen standing before the angel of the Lord, appearing, that is to say, before Jehovah as the representative of the people and officiating before Him; and the guilty fears of the people find a mouthpiece in Satan, who stands resisting Joshua's intercession on the ground of the past transgressions of the people. This was precisely what the thoughtful and conscience-stricken minds among the Jews conceived to be going on in the presence-chamber of Jehovah. The vision was designed to remove these fears, by showing that the sin which Joshua bore as their representative was removed, his ministry accepted, and the priesthood established anew.

1. *And he showed me*, that is, the interpreting angel showed me, *Joshua the high priest standing before the angel of the Lord*. The expression "standing before" is equally applicable to a prisoner at the bar of his judge, and to a priest ministering in presence of the Divinity. As the person here spoken of is a priest, the latter meaning at once suggests itself as appropriate; but the mention of the accuser and the other adjuncts of the scene point rather to the former. Indeed, the filthy state of the priest's dress almost necessarily excludes the idea that he is entering God's presence to minister. In any case, he stands before *the angel of the Lord*, or **the angel who represents Jehovah**, as the representative of the people, and the sins that stain him are the people's sins; and the case to be tried is, whether he, as the people's representative and priest, is to be accepted or rejected. This appears from ver. 2, in which Satan is rebuked in the name of "the Lord that hath chosen," not Joshua, but "Jerusalem;" as well as from ver. 9, in which it is affirmed that the iniquity of the *land* shall be removed. The vision shows "*Satan standing at his right hand to resist him:*" lit. **the accuser standing at his right hand** to accuse him, the Satan standing in the position commonly occupied by the plaintiff in a Jewish court of law (cp. Ps. cix. 6). The word *Satan* is translated in the N. T. by two words, both of which are borrowed from courts of law.

2. Satan is rebuked by *the Lord that hath chosen Jerusalem*, because this choice (ii. 12) and the ultimate design of it are contradicted and opposed by Satan's attempt to induce God to cast off His people. "Who shall lay anything to the charge of God's elect?" The same idea is involved in the next clause, *Is not this a brand plucked out of the fire?* Charred and unsightly as the bit of timber may be, the fact of its being plucked out of the fire proves its value to the owner, and that he sees a further purpose it can serve. The fire in this case was the captivity from which the people had been rescued. The figure was used earlier by Amos (iv. 11), and graphically sets before the mind the quick eagerness with which an article

3 the fire? Now Joshua was clothed with filthy garments, and
4 stood before the angel. And he answered and spake unto those that stood before him, saying, Take away the filthy garments from him. And unto him he said, Behold, I have caused thine iniquity to pass from thee, and I will clothe
5 thee with change of raiment. And I said, Let them set a fair mitre upon his head. So they set a fair mitre upon his head, and clothed him with garments. And the angel of the
6 LORD stood by. And the angel of the LORD protested unto
7 Joshua, saying, Thus saith the LORD of hosts; If thou wilt walk in my ways, and if thou wilt keep my charge, then thou shalt also judge my house, and shalt also keep my courts, and I will give thee places to walk among these that stand by.

of value is snatched from a destruction to which it is exposed. (A bank-note that has been thrown into the fire as waste-paper; or a letter from which we have forgotten to copy an expression or an address, and which is snatched out half burnt.)

3. *Filthy garments*, exhibiting Joshua's unfitness to enter God's presence as the high priest. In general, such clothing symbolizes the defilement of sin (cp. next verse; Isa. lxiv. 6; Rev. iii. 4). Filthy garments make a man unpleasant company. They make him offensive, disgusting, possibly contagious to others; and if he has not lost all sense of decency, they are to himself a source of shame and discomfort. Sin is similarly a bar to intercourse with God. Some conversation is so foul and some sins so abominable that even decent men turn quickly away in disgust: but to God all sin is foul and hideous.

4. *Change of raiment*, **splendid, festival raiment**, corresponding to our *dress clothes, holiday attire,* or *court dress,* and symbolic not of mere purity, but of jubilant welcome and joyful fellowship with God. Observe it is God, the angel of Jehovah, who gives the change of raiment. Joshua could do nothing to cleanse or cover his stained clothes (see Questions).

5. *And I said*, that is, I Zechariah. The mitre is described in Ex. xxviii. 36. It bore a gold plate across the forehead with the inscription, "Holiness to the Lord." The priest was to wear it that the services of the people "might be accepted before the Lord." It was significant of the forgiveness of the sins of holy things.

6, 7. The solemn protestation with which God here renews the covenant of the priesthood is composed of balanced clauses: *If thou wilt* **walk** *in my ways, I will give thee places* to **walk** *among these that stand by. If thou wilt* **keep** *my charge, thou shalt also* **keep** *my courts.* To "judge my house" means to regulate the temple services, and discharge all the functions of the priesthood; to be supreme in God's house. "*Places to walk among these that stand by*" means free access to my presence among those who surround my throne. Instead of being an outcast, and afraid to enter the presence chamber, Joshua will be freely admitted to the presence as the recognised and accepted representative of God's people; he will have his place among those who are most familiarly known in the heavenly court.

8 Hear now, O Joshua the high priest, thou, and thy fellows that sit before thee: for they *are* men wondered at: for, 9 behold, I will bring forth my servant the BRANCH. For behold the stone that I have laid before Joshua; upon one stone *shall be* seven eyes: behold, I will engrave the graving thereof, saith the LORD of hosts, and I will remove the 10 iniquity of that land in one day. In that day, saith the

8. *Hear now;* the announcement to which their attention is directed appears to be "*for, behold . . . the Branch.*" Those who are summoned to listen are the high priest and his assessors in council, *thou and thy fellows that sit before thee.* The standing "council of the temple," which regulated everything connected with the affairs and services of the sanctuary, consisted of fourteen members, the high priest, his suffragan (the Sagan), two chief treasurers, three under treasurers, and seven "Ammarcalin," who had charge of all the gates (Edersheim, *Temple,* p. 75). But it is unlikely that this council was complete in Zechariah's time. The reason given for making this announcement to them is that *they are men wondered at:* lit. men of **miracle, sign, portent,** and usually understood to mean typical men, men who foreshadow some more perfect sanctuary and service. Our translators seem to have had in view the idea that Joshua's colleagues, as well as himself, were *wonderful* instances of God's forgiving and restoring grace. The translation of the LXX. is much simpler: **they are capable of reading signs, of interpreting marvels.** This was part of the priest's function, and to them, therefore, the announcement is made which it would have been useless to make to men not accustomed to interpret signs and symbols. *I will bring forth my servant the Branch:* lit. I bring my servant Tsemach. From the absence of the article one would suppose that this title had now become a proper name. It is first found as a designation of the Messiah in Isa. iv. 2 (cp. Jer. xxiii. 5; Ps. lxxx. 15; Isa. xi. 10), in which passage it would appear that the idea originating the title was that the Messiah was the grand result which God looked for from Israel, the fruit-bearing branch which would compensate for the barrenness of the rest. Other passages more directly point to the idea that out of the stem of Jesse, out of the Davidic stock, now so marred and truncated, there would one day spring a branch in which the whole family should be glorified.

9. The *stone* may either be **the foundation-stone** of the temple which had been **laid in presence of Joshua** some years before this, or the stone laid when the building was resumed at Haggai's instigation, or most probably it was a stone yet lying in the hewer's shed, known by the people because it had been selected for its dimensions or beauty to serve as the topstone of the building. The *seven eyes* are in chap. iv. interpreted as "the eyes of the Lord which run to and fro through the whole earth," and therefore symbolize the universal providence of God which was to be exercised in behalf of this stone. (The number seven was expressive of perfection; cp. especially Ezra vii. 14, and see note on iv. 10.) The stone was selected, but not yet hewn and carved, and the people were probably despairing of its ever being so; therefore the promise, *I will engrave the graving thereof;* in other words, I **will have a hand in every detail of this building.** *In one day,* **in a short time,** either **soon or suddenly.**

10. This verse depicts the peace and prosperity that would ensue when

Lord of hosts, shall ye call every man his neighbour under the vine and under the fig tree.

these preceding promises were fulfilled (cp. Micah iv. 4, and 1 Kings iv. 25).

Contrast with ver. 2 *the story of Althaia and the burning brand; and show the applicability of the expression "a brand plucked out of the fire" to a person who has formed habits or entered upon courses the natural and common results of which are destructive, but who has yet been rescued from the full experience of these results.*
What were the characteristic garments of the high priest? On what occasion was he arrayed in plain white? What was the shape of the mitre, and whence?
How can God remove our sin, its guilt and its cause? Can He remove the shame that follows wrong-doing? "No true penitent forgets or forgives himself"—is that true?
What were the duties of the temple watch? Explain Rev. xvi. 15. [*When one of the temple watch was found asleep, his garments were set on fire.*]
Subjects for teachers to enlarge upon: Significance of clothes; of priestly dress; different customs of East and West about wearing hat and shoes in holy places. From the word "charge" (ver. 7) explain "car," "cargo," to "charge" a gun, a jury, an enemy. What is a bishop's charge? And what in strictness does "charger" mean?

CHAPTER IV.

1 And the angel that talked with me came again, and waked

Fifth Vision: The Golden Candlestick (iv. 1–14).

Object of the Vision.—The preceding vision was meant to reinstate the religious head of the nation; this is meant to give Zerubbabel, the civil head, the assurance that he also is God's anointed, endowed with power from God to do God's work, as truly as ever any of his royal forefathers had been. By means of God's favour shown to these two heads of the people, the church will shine again as a light in the world. The prophet had looked with dismay at the half-built temple, he had heard the wind howling through the unsheltered area where the candlestick should have been erected; he had taken the measure of Zerubbabel, and fancied no great work would ever be done by such a man; he had begun to think of the Church of God as a failure, its light blown out, its very pedestal upset, but this vision recalls him to better thoughts, to the purpose of God regarding His church. God, he sees, means to re-establish His Church in all its former glory. This weak, incompetent Zerubbabel, born a captive, and showing the craven spirit of a captive, would be animated by God's Spirit, and would be a worthy head to the people.

1. *Waked me.* These visions were seen by night, probably while Zechariah

2 me, as a man that is wakened out of his sleep, And said unto me, What seest thou? And I said, I have looked, and behold a candlestick all *of* gold, with a bowl upon the top of it, and his seven lamps thereon, and seven pipes to the
3 seven lamps, which *are* upon the top thereof: And two olive trees by it, one upon the right *side* of the bowl, and the
4 other upon the left *side* thereof. So I answered and spake to the angel that talked with me, saying, What *are* these, my
5 lord? Then the angel that talked with me answered and said unto me, Knowest thou not what these be? And I said,
6 No, my lord. Then he answered and spake unto me, saying, This *is* the word of the LORD unto Zerubbabel, saying, Not by might, nor by power, but by my spirit, saith

slept, but so vivid were they that he seemed "as a man that is wakened." The angel stirred him to so keen an attention that he can best express it by saying "he waked me."

2. *A candlestick.* The tabernacle being a tent, without windows, artificial light was requisite. This was provided for by the lamp described in Ex. xxv. 31, similar in form to the one now seen by Zechariah, and probably reproduced in that which is figured on the Arch of Titus, in which the seven lights are in one perpendicular plane. The original candelabra, however, not only served a practical purpose, but formed a part of the symbolism of the tabernacle. As in the vision of John (Rev. i.) the seven candlesticks which he saw are explained to be seven churches; so this combination of lights in the tabernacle (and temple) symbolized the whole Church or people of God which was set to shine as a light in the world. It is, indeed, only in the Head of the Church that the symbolism finds its reality; it is only from Christ that perfect knowledge of God flows forth to men; but as He says of Himself "I am the light of the world," so also He says to His people "Ye are the light of the world."

[Note that the light which symbolizes the knowledge of God, is not the sun or any natural light, but an artificial light supplied with a specially-prepared oil. For the knowledge of God is, in truth, not natural nor common to all men, but furnished over and above nature.] *Seven pipes to the seven lamps:* lit. **seven and seven pipes to the lamps**, which would mean seven pipes to each lamp, denoting a perfect fulness of communication. It is a visionary candlestick.

3. *Two olive trees.* This forms the distinctive feature of the candlestick here seen. It was supplied not from a vessel of oil but from two living trees. In other words, the supply of oil was perennial and inexhaustible. The bowls might be small, but the source from which they might be refilled was a living fountain of oil (see on ver. 14).

6. *This is the word of the Lord*, *i.e.* **This is God's way of saying to Zerubbabel.** What the vision did say then follows: *Not by might*, etc. You have taken your own measure, you feel your weakness to cope with your circumstances, you are painfully conscious of your inability to shine and scatter the surrounding darkness; but you are to understand that it is God's Spirit who is the source of every brilliant and enlightening action that reflects glory upon

7 the LORD of hosts. Who *art* thou, O great mountain? before Zerubbabel *thou shalt become* a plain: and he shall bring forth the headstone *thereof with* shoutings, *crying,*
8 Grace, grace unto it. Moreover the word of the LORD came
9 unto me, saying, The hands of Zerubbabel have laid the foundation of this house; his hands shall also finish it; and thou shalt know that the LORD of hosts hath sent me unto
10 you. For who hath despised the day of small things? for they shall rejoice, and shall see the plummet in the hand of Zerubbabel *with* those seven; they *are* the eyes of the LORD,
11 which run to and fro through the whole earth. Then answered I, and said unto him, What *are* these two olive trees upon the right *side* of the candlestick and upon the left *side* thereof?
12 And I answered again, and said unto him, What be *these* two olive branches which through the two golden pipes empty the
13 golden *oil* out of themselves? And he answered me and said, Knowest thou not what these *be?* And I said, No, my lord.
14 Then said he, These *are* the two anointed ones, that stand by the Lord of the whole earth.

God. You have not to create a holy spirit in yourself. Holiness sufficient for the need of all creatures exists in God. As there is in God life enough to uphold all creatures in life, so there is in Him holiness sufficient for every good thing that needs to be done. You can never find yourself face to face with any duty for which there is not grace enough. In yourself there may be far too little, but in God is a living fountain.

7. *O great mountain.* All the obstacles that had risen up before Zerubbabel's fears, and been magnified by him into enormous dimensions (cp. Jer. li. 25; Matt. xxi. 21), would be overcome. The *headstone* of the temple would at last be brought out of the hewer's shed with shouts of triumph both from the builders and the assembled crowd, and with earnest prayer that God would show **favour** ("*grace*") to this finished work, and would long keep that stone in its place.

10. *For they shall rejoice,* etc., or, **they see with joy the plummet in the hand of Zerubbabel, even those seven, the eyes of the Lord.** Those eyes which see everything in the world (cp. Milton's *Paradise Lost,* iii. 648) rest with greatest complacency on the topstone of the temple and Zerubbabel fitting it into its place, plummet in hand (cp. ceremonies at laying of foundation-stones among ourselves by great personages; African custom of slaughtering slaves, and laying their bodies under foundations).

12. *What be these two olive branches,* etc., better, **What are the two olive branches at the side of the two golden tubes which empty the golden [oil] out of themselves** (cp. Rev. xi. 4).

14. *The two anointed ones:* lit. **two sons of oil.** Priest and king in Israel were set apart to their office by anointing. The two *trees* are the royalty and priesthood; the two *branches* are their present representatives, Joshua and Zerubbabel. Through these two, that is, through the prosperous administra-

tion of things civil and religious, God will enable His people to triumph over present difficulties and shine in the world. And it is precisely in proportion as Christians practically use Christ as their king and priest that they receive His Spirit. They who, in the bitter consciousness of the wasted life that lies behind them, turn to God for forgiveness and for strength to do the will of Christ, do certainly receive the Almighty, Living Spirit to renew and strengthen them.

Specify the difficulties with which Zerubbabel had to contend.
When did Zerubbabel lay the foundation of the temple? What is the word "plummet" derived from? What is a "Lesbian rule"? What are the tools now used by one who lays a foundation-stone?
Collect N. T. passages illustrative of the position occupied respectively by Christ and Christians as stones in the Church. Explain the expressions "corner-stone," "lively stones," "edify," "the stone which the builders rejected is become the head of the corner."
What are the conditions which must be observed if Christians are to shine as lights? What feature in this vision gives assurance that for the right discharge of every duty, and for right conduct in all circumstances, there is grace enough prepared?
Give other instances of the use of the idiom used in the expression "sons of oil."
Why are "olive" trees specified as feeding the lamp?
On what plea are candles now used in worship by Ritualists?

CHAPTER V.

1 THEN I turned, and lifted up mine eyes, and looked, and

SIXTH AND SEVENTH VISIONS: THE FLYING ROLL AND THE WOMAN IN THE EPHAH (v. 1-11).

Object of the Vision.—The object of both the visions recorded in this chapter was to encourage God's people to expect that the land would be cleansed from evil-doers and wickedness. The previous visions had assured the prophet that all civil and ecclesiastical advantages would be given to the people; but at once it would occur to him to think, What avails this reformed state, if the people themselves remain as they were before they were swept out of their land? It was to meet this disheartening thought that these visions were sent.

1. *A flying roll*, or sheet of parchment or other substance prepared for writing on. It would have somewhat the appearance of a wall map. Roll is a literal translation of the Hebrew word *Megillah*, which was gradually appropriated to the five books, Ruth, Esther, Lamentations, Canticles, and Ecclesiastes; and subsequently to the book of Esther by pre-eminence (cp. the process by which the word denoting any *books* has come to signify *the books*, the Bible). The roll was *flying*, to denote its swift, unembarrassed pursuit of its object; like a bird of prey, as Reuss says.

2 behold a flying roll. And he said unto me, What seest thou? And I answered, I see a flying roll; the length thereof *is* 3 twenty cubits, and the breadth thereof ten cubits. Then said he unto me, This *is* the curse that goeth forth over the face of the whole earth: for every one that stealeth shall be cut off *as* on this side according to it; and every one that sweareth 4 shall be cut off *as* on that side according to it. I will bring it forth, saith the LORD of hosts, and it shall enter into the house of the thief, and into the house of him that sweareth falsely by my name: and it shall remain in the midst of his house, and shall consume it with the timber thereof and the 5 stones thereof. Then the angel that talked with me went forth, and said unto me, Lift up now thine eyes, and see what 6 *is* this that goeth forth. And I said, What *is* it? And he said, This *is* an ephah that goeth forth. He said moreover, This

2. *The length . . . cubits.* This was the apparent size as the prophet saw it in the air. These dimensions are intended to convey the impression of unusual magnitude, as of a roll capable of containing a great multitude of specified offences. (Hebrew measures of length were the finger's breadth, the hand-breadth, the span, the cubit, the reed.)

3. *Earth,* better, **land.** *Shall be cut off as on this side according to it,* better, **shall be driven** (lit. purged, cleaned out, cleansed away) hence **according to it.** The last word might be rendered **like it,** which would point to the rapid flight of the curse as the image of the rapid banishment of the wicked; the other meaning is preferable. *Every one that sweareth* is, as the next verse shows, **every perjured person.** Possibly the curse on the roll was aimed chiefly at those who kept back money from the fund for rebuilding the temple, and swore they had none to spare. The two sins are frequently united; as when a person falsely fills up and signs his income-tax schedule.

4. This verse is illustrated by the story of Glaucus (*Herod.* vi. 85), who had received a deposit of money in trust, but when it was demanded back, sought to appropriate it. With this object in view, he asked the oracle at Delphi if he might take an oath he had never received it. He received the following answer:—

" Best for the present it were, O Glaucus, to do as thou wishest,
Swearing an oath to prevail, and so to make prize of the money.
Swear then—death is the lot ev'n of those who never swear falsely.
Yet hath the Oath-God a son, nameless, footless, and handless;
Mighty in strength he approaches to vengeance and whelms in destruction
All who belong to the race, or the house of the man who is perjured."

The curse is to take up its abode with the sinner till all about him is consumed, his name and place blotted out.

6. *Ephah.* A measure containing upwards of three pecks or seven gallons; the largest in actual use among the Jews. In this, wickedness is conveyed away; not in a mere box or cage; evidently denoting that the wickedness of the people was an ascertained quantity, that all the sins of individuals, the petty cheatings and white lies and plausible statements had all gone into an

7 *is* their resemblance through all the earth. And, behold, there was lifted up a talent of lead: and this *is* a woman that
8 sitteth in the midst of the ephah. And he said, This *is* wickedness. And he cast it into the midst of the ephah; and
9 he cast the weight of lead upon the mouth thereof. Then lifted I up mine eyes, and looked, and, behold, there came out two women, and the wind *was* in their wings; for they had wings like the wings of a stork: and they lifted up the
10 ephah between the earth and the heaven. Then said I to the angel that talked with me, Whither do these bear the
11 ephah? And he said unto me, To build it an house in the land of Shinar: and it shall be established, and set there upon her own base.

accurate standard measure. The word translated *resemblance* is thought by some to be an error in transcription for the word denoting *iniquity*, and this gives a better sense, "**This is the iniquity of all the land,**" but there is no call to change the present reading.

7. *Talent of lead*, lit. a circle of lead. The secondary meaning of the word was a talent, which was a weight for metals and weighed over a *cwt*. This heavy circular cover lay on the ephah to keep the contents from spilling; to keep down the struggling resisting wickedness.

8. Wickedness is represented by a woman; as are merchandise, music, poetry, or any of the nationalities. (Why?) This symbol presents wickedness as full-grown, seductive, plotting, prolific, but also as separable from the life and customs of the people with which it had seemed inextricably involved.

The weight of lead, lit. **the stone of lead**; because stones were anciently used as weights (cp. our own word *stone*).

9. *The wind was in their wings*. They soared and sailed on the breeze as large-winged birds on a windy day, without effort. This was easy to them, as they *had wings like the wings of a stork*, a bird whose long black wings stretching out from its white body have not only a striking and beautiful effect, but enable it to fly immense distances. In its annual migration it covers a longer distance than from Jerusalem to Shinar (cp. Tristram).

10. *Shinar*. Cp. Gen. xi. 2; the land in which men first deliberately conspired against God, and sought to protect themselves against Him, as if He were a demon—a land fit only for transporting convicts to. The ephah shall be set there, so as to secure that it and its contents never return to holy land.

REMARKS.—1. The visions may be entitled, **The Cleansing of the Land**, or, **The Banishment of Wickedness**.

2. The prosperity of a community depends not only on outward tokens of God's favour, good harvests, absence of epidemics, success in war or diplomacy; nor only on the possession of a good government and an ecclesiastical condition of which neither radical nor conservative can complain; but mainly on the sound moral character of the people. Build a house with every appliance for comfort, finish it in the best style, and then invite into it a family that has been used to a hovel, and your fine house will soon be filthy and uninhabit-

able. Put a foolish, incompetent, pleasure-seeking lad into a good-going business, and he will soon wreck both it and himself. God prepares a heaven for us, but we by our very entrance into it make it a hell.

3. The subtle, impalpable, searching, inevitable, consuming nature of the curse. It cannot be shut out : it cannot be resisted. It steals in like a pestilence. It passes like dry-rot or a fire from timber to timber till all is consumed.

4. The ancient custom of cleansing the land by banishing or slaying the criminal, and our modern system of transportation.

What sins would you specify as now needing to be packed up and banished?
What words in our language link us to the time when books and records were "rolls"? In what words of ours does the memory of the old materials of books (bark, papyrus, skins) live on?
What is the etymological significance of the words cubit, stork, talent, parchment, Bible?
What passage in Scripture shows that a talent of silver was about as much as a man could carry?
Illustrate the cleansing of the land from the book of Revelation, and compare the work of King Arthur:

" As now
Men weed the white horse on the Berkshire hills
To keep him bright and clean as heretofore,
He rooted out the slothful officer.
    .   .   .   .   .
Clear'd the dark places and let in the law.
And broke the bandit's holds and cleansed the land "

CHAPTER VI.

1 AND I turned, and lifted up mine eyes, and looked, and, behold, there came four chariots out from between two moun-

EIGHTH VISION : THE FOUR WAR-CHARIOTS (vi. 1-8).

Object of the Vision.—To convey the assurance that the re-established order and peace of Israel, depicted in the foregoing visions, would not again be disturbed by the powers which had hitherto molested and oppressed God's people. Babylonia and Egypt especially would be visited by such divine judgments as should appease the Spirit of God aroused to anger by the sufferings of Israel.

1. *Four chariots.* Chariots being among the most formidable of ancient military engines, and being also used on great state occasions, came to be symbolic of authority and of resistless might (cp. Ps. lxviii. 17 ; Isa. lxvi. 15 ; Hab. iii. 8 ; Hag. ii. 22). Those seen by Zechariah are explained in ver. 5 as representing the winds, which again themselves represent the invisible mighty agencies sent forth by God to accomplish His purpose (cp. Ps. civ. 3,

2 tains; and the mountains *were* mountains of brass. In the
first chariot *were* red horses; and in the second chariot black
3 horses; And in the third chariot white horses; and in the
4 fourth chariot grisled and bay horses. Then I answered and
said unto the angel that talked with me, What *are* these, my
5 lord? And the angel answered and said unto me, These *are*
the four spirits of the heavens, which go forth from standing
6 before the Lord of all the earth. The black horses which *are*
therein go forth into the north country; and the white go
forth after them; and the grisled go forth toward the south
7 country. And the bay went forth, and sought to go that they
might walk to and fro through the earth: and he said, Get
you hence, walk to and fro through the earth. So they

"who maketh the clouds His chariot; who walketh upon the wings of the wind; who maketh the winds His messengers"; see also Ps. cxlviii. 8, and Dan. vii. 2). They are four, because God's agents are sent to every quarter.

From between two mountains . . . of brass. "From a formidable and inaccessible gorge, that is to say, from the very abode of God" (Reuss), as if from a strongly-intrenched and impregnable seat of government. The Hebrew has the article, "**the two mountains**," so that Zion and the Mount of Olives may have been in the prophet's mind, as both are prophetic symbols of the source of judgment (cp. Joel iii. 2, 12, 16; Zech. xiv. 4), and Jerusalem is thus represented as the point of departure of God's judgments. But the may only show us that already the prophet had seen the mountains, but in the rapidity of narration omits to say so.

2. *Red horses.* Neither here nor in the first chapter does the prophet explain the various colours, but he probably attached to them the usual significance—red representing blood and carnage; black, famine and mourning; white, victory; grisled, mixed fortunes. [But as the word rendered "*grisled*" etymologically means **spotted as with a hail-shower**, Hengstenberg sees an allusion to judgments falling like a storm of hail (cp. Rev. viii. 7; and especially Rev. xvi. 21).]

3. *Grisled and bay*, lit. **spotted, vigorous.** In the Hebrew *and* is not represented, and the word rendered *bay* means **active**, or **nimble.** Some scholars, however, think it may mean **bright red**, and therefore translate the whole expression **spotted red**; in a word, **roan.** [*Grisled*, from the French *gris*, grey; now spelt *grizzled*.]

5. *These are the four . . . the Lord.* It is doubtful whether *spirits* might not rather be translated **winds**, but the words following represent them as going forth from presenting themselves before the Lord, and therefore indicate a conscious energy. Perhaps the most instructive parallel is Rev. vii. 1.

6. *North country.* The north country is **Babylonia**; the south country, Egypt (cp. Jer. xxv. 9, also i. 14, 15. For the combination of Babylon and Egypt, see Isa. vii. 18). Observe that two teams go to the north; Babylonia is doubly smitten (Reuss).

7. *The bay.* In the distribution of the chariots, the prophet makes no mention of the red horses, and to make up the number, four, divides the grisled

8 walked to and fro through the earth. Then cried he upon me, and spake unto me, saying, Behold, these that go toward the north country have quieted my spirit in the north country.

9, 10 And the word of the LORD came unto me, saying, Take of *them* of the captivity, *even* of Heldai, of Tobijah, and of Jedaiah, which are come from Babylon, and come thou the

and bay into two separate teams. Critics, however, suspect there is a clerical error, and that we should read "*red*" in place of "*bay*." Though two countries are specified, no part of the earth was to be exempt from the evidences of God's righteous government.

8. *Quieted my spirit*, lit. "**have caused my spirit to rest**," apparently equivalent to "**have pacified my spirit**" (cp. Ezek. v. 13, and xvi. 42). Judgment having been inflicted on Babylon, the anger of the Lord would no more be roused against it.

> *Sketch the fulfilment of this prophecy in Babylonia and Egypt. Justify God's taking vengeance on these countries.* ["*The truest benevolence is occasional severity. Else, why pestilence, famine, Cromwell and Perrot in Ireland, Charlemagne hanging 4000 Saxons over the Weser Bridge; did not God bless these terrible righteous judgments?* . . . *Recollect how before the '89 men were maundering about universal peace and philanthropy, too loving to hate God's enemies, too indulgent to punish sin.*" *Recollect that and what succeeded.*]
> *What is the difference between the use of "my spirit," here and in the N. T.; what operations are ascribed in O. T. to the Spirit of God which we should now ascribe simply to God; and what are in O. T. ascribed to God which we should ascribe to the Spirit?*
> *What is the radical meaning of "spirit;" also of "ghost," and "animal"? God being a Spirit, why is one person of the Trinity called by preeminence the Spirit? What is the meaning of "our ghostly enemy," and of Shakespeare's words, "Hence will I to my ghostly father's cell"?*

THE CROWNING OF JOSHUA (vi. 9–15).

A deputation from the Jews remaining in Babylonia seems to have arrived in Jerusalem with contributions in aid of the rebuilding of the temple. This was an event both immediately encouraging and typical of far larger aid and ingathering. Zechariah is instructed to make crowns of the gold and silver they had brought, and, having first set them on the head of Joshua, to lay them up in the temple as a memorial or pledge that those who were far off would come to the temple of the Lord and enjoy the advantages of the crowned priest's government.

9. Probably this message came to the prophet immediately after he had seen the visions.

10–11. *Take of them* . . . *silver and gold:* lit. **Take from the captivity, from Heldai, from Tobijah** . . . **and come thou this day, and come into**

same day, and go into the house of Josiah the son of
11 Zephaniah; Then take silver and gold, and make crowns,
and set *them* upon the head of Joshua the son of Josedech,
12 the high priest; And speak unto him, saying, Thus
speaketh the LORD of hosts, saying, Behold the man whose
name *is* The BRANCH; and he shall grow up out of his
13 place, and he shall build the temple of the LORD: Even he

the house of Josiah the son of Zephaniah, and take silver and gold. The
"*take*" of ver. 11 resumes the sentence begun with the "take" of ver. 10,
which is in a different construction, and might, perhaps, be better translated,
As to taking. It is an injunction to accept the gifts brought from Babylon
by these men (all of whom, as Pusey remarks, have names compounded with
Jah, expressing the faith of the exiles in their God), and instruction regarding
the use to be made of a part of the gold and silver they had brought. He is
to go to the house of Josiah, as the deputies were apparently living as his
guests. The *captivity* is the term used by Jeremiah (xxix. 20, 31), and by
Ezekiel (iii. 11), to denote those who had been carried captive. (Ezra continues to use the term of those who had returned to their own land.)
Crowns. The word is plural, but it is doubtful whether it means two
separate crowns. In Job xxxi. 36 it is translated **crown**; and in verse 14 it
is followed by a verb in the singular. The crowns symbolic of different
sovereignties are sometimes wrought into one so as to be worn at once by the
same person (cp. Rev. xix. 12. The double crown of Egypt, the *pschent*, was
always placed on the king's head at his coronation, representing his
sovereignty over Upper and Lower Egypt. See Wilkinson, iii. 351; Edwards'
Thousand Miles up the Nile, i. 169). The significance of the act does not
consist in the nature of the crown, but in the material of which it was made,—
the gold and silver of those who were far away from Jerusalem,—and in the
person upon whose head it was set. The crown is set on Joshua: no crown
is set on Zerubbabel. "It would have been confusing; a seeming restoration
of the kingdom when it was not to be restored; an encouragement of the
temporal hopes, which were the bane of Israel" (Pusey). By placing the
symbol of royalty on the head of the priest, Zechariah shows that the kingdom of the Branch—of Him in whom David's kingdom is to come to its
fullest development—is not to be a kingdom of this world. The proclamation (ver. 12) which accompanied the coronation explains its typical
significance.

12. *Behold the man:* lit. **Behold a man, Branch is his name** (*i.e.* **whose
name is Branch.** The word rendered *branch* signifies rather a **shoot** or
sprout). The Branch was already an accepted title of the Messiah (cp. iii. 8),
and Branch (*Tsemach*) was used as a proper name. It would therefore be
readily understood that Joshua, as he stood a crowned priest, was a picture of
what the Messiah was to be. *And he shall grow up out of his place:* lit. **And
from under him he shall sprout** (or, **there shall be sprouting**). His name
is Shoot, and he shall shoot up from his place or root. The words indicate
the vital energy of the shoot. They also, perhaps, point to the self-sustaining
character of the shoot, and to its place being already defined in the mind of
God.

13. *Even he shall build.* This reiteration is to call attention. Zerubbabel

shall build the temple of the LORD; and he shall bear the
glory, and shall sit and rule upon his throne; and he shall
be a priest upon his throne: and the counsel of peace shall
14 be between them both. And the crowns shall be to Helem,
and to Tobijah, and to Jedaiah, and to Hen the son of
15 Zephaniah, for a memorial in the temple of the LORD. And
they *that are* far off shall come and build in the temple of the
LORD, and ye shall know that the LORD of hosts hath sent me
unto you. And *this* shall come to pass, if ye will diligently
obey the voice of the LORD your God.

had been assured he was to complete the rebuilding of the temple. The
temple now spoken of must therefore either be another, or there must be
some glory which can be given to the temple only by the Messianic Priest
(Eph. ii. 22). *Counsel of peace*, government of which a happy condition is the
outcome. *Shall be between them both.* Who or what are the two alluded to?
The simplest translation and interpretation seem to be: *Branch . . . shall sit
and rule upon his throne*, **and there shall be a priest upon his throne, and
the counsel of peace shall be between them both,** *i.e.* between Branch and
the priest. The rule of Branch shall not abolish the priestly rule, but confirm
it. But there is no insuperable objection to the more usual interpretation:
Branch shall bear both the royal dignity and the priestly, and these two
working harmoniously will produce sound government. So that the meaning
is substantially the same as that given by the vision of the candlestick, that it
is through the kingly and priestly offices that God blesses His people. The
fulfilment of this in our Lord is obvious.

14. *Helem*, the same person as Heldai, ver. 10; as *Hen* is supposed to be
the same as Josiah. Others prefer to render *Hen* not as a proper name, but as
"favour," **the favour of the son of Zephaniah.** (The LXX. do so; indeed,
they treat the other proper names also in the same way.) This would imply
that the crowns were laid up as a memorial of the hospitality shown by
Josiah to the deputation. But why so ordinary an act of courtesy should
be so extraordinarily rewarded is not explained. The crowns were in any
case to be **to Helem**, and the others **for a memorial**, as a memento of
their liberality, and as if perpetually to remind God of those who though
distant from Jerusalem regarded it as their home, and its God as their God
(cp. Ex. xxviii. 12; Num. x. 10; Acts x. 4). This laying up of a memorial
shows that the Messianic time was not immediately expected. The crowns
were to serve as a standing representation of the dispersion, and as the pledge
of that ingathering of which this deputation was an earnest (cp. ver. 15).

Give other instances of symbolic action by the prophets.
*Give historical examples of double or triple crowns. What is the technical
name of a bishop's throne? What does Milton mean by the line,
"New Presbyter is but Old Priest writ large"? and by the other line
in the same ode, "And ride us with a classic hierarchy"? And
why have men generally objected to priestly rule?*
*Specify other predictions in which the Messiah is represented as combining
royalty and priesthood.*

Why did the Jews so pride themselves in their temple? Do the dispensations go back or advance? Attractiveness of temple-building; how we can assist in it; encouragements to believe that many now far off shall be drawn nigh.

CHAPTER VII.

1 AND it came to pass in the fourth year of king Darius, *that* the word of the LORD came unto Zechariah in the fourth
2 day of the ninth month, *even* in Chisleu; When they had sent unto the house of God Sherezer and Regem-melech, and

THE DECISION REGARDING FAST-DAYS (vii. and viii.).

During the captivity the Jews had been accustomed to observe certain fasts in acknowledgment of their afflicted condition and its cause. One of these fasts had been appointed to commemorate and bewail the destruction of Jerusalem by Nebuchadnezzar. It struck the men of Bethel that this fast was now out of place as the restored city and temple daily assumed more promising proportions. They were intelligent and honest men, who felt that a religious service which was not the expression of present feeling but a mere antiquated observance was worse than useless. At the same time, they had too much respect for ecclesiastical authority to take upon themselves to abolish the fast-day. They therefore sent a deputation, headed by Sherezer and Regem-melech, to inquire whether it was the mind of Jehovah that they should retain this fast. This gives occasion for a full treatment both of the general subject of fasting and of the days set apart for it. The response may be thus divided:—
(1) Obedience is better than fasting (vers. 4–7).
(2) Disobedience lay at the root of all their past misery (vers. 8–14).
(3) But now, according to the days wherein they had seen evil, so would the Lord make them glad (viii. 1–17).
(4) Fasts shall be turned into feasts (18–23).

1. *In the fourth year of King Darius*, B.C. 518, nearly two years subsequent to the visions and the resumption of building. The month *Chisleu* most nearly corresponded to our December. (The word means **stiff, frozen**; as Abib means *sprouting*; Ziv, *blossoming*, and so on; cp. the French names *Brumaire, Frimaire, Nivose, Germinal*, given to the months by the Republic.)
2. *When they had sent unto the house of God Sherezer and Regem-melech, and their men*, rather, **when Bethel had sent Sherezer and Regem-melech, and their men.** *Bethel* is never used for the temple, but only as the name of a place, a town. In the next verse the temple is called *the house of the Lord*. (There is, however, nothing in the construction to prevent it meaning, when Bethel, Sherezer, and Regem-melech, and their people sent.) Sherezer was an Assyrian name, meaning *prince of fire*. It was the name of one of Sennacherib's parricidal sons. See 2 Kings xix. 37. *Regem-melech* means

3 their men, to pray before the LORD, *And* to speak unto the priests which *were* in the house of the LORD of hosts, and to the prophets, saying, Should I weep in the fifth month, separating myself, as I have done these so many years?
4 Then came the word of the LORD of hosts unto me, saying,
5 Speak unto all the people of the land, and to the priests, saying, When ye fasted and mourned in the fifth and seventh *month*, even those seventy years, did ye at all fast unto me,
6 *even* to me? And when ye did eat, and when ye did drink,
7 did not ye eat *for yourselves*, and drink *for yourselves?* *Should ye* not *hear* the words which the LORD hath cried by the former prophets, when Jerusalem was inhabited and in prosperity, and the cities thereof round about her, when *men*

friend of the king. To pray before the Lord, rather, **to propitiate the Lord:** lit. **to stroke the face of Jehovah;** an anthropomorphic expression derived from the idea of caressing, stroking the face to smooth away the wrinkles of displeasure; precisely as the Latin *palpare* is used ["quem munere palpat," *Juv.* i. 35].

3. *Should I weep . . . separating myself*, or, **Shall I weep, abstaining.** (The word translated *separating myself* is the root from which is derived **Nazarite**, one who vows abstinence, a consecrated person.) Observe that the question is put to the priests *and to the prophets*. It was the fast *in the fifth month* which was especially burdensome. There were altogether four fasts (chap. viii. 19), in the fourth, fifth, seventh, and tenth months. The fast in the fifth month commemorated the destruction of the city and temple by Nebuchadnezzar, as related in Jer. lii. 12-14. [In the account of the same event given in 2 Kings xxv. 8, the seventh and not the tenth day of the fifth month is given as the date. The city may, perhaps, have been three days in flames.] It was this fast which now seemed most out of place in presence of the restored temple. It is well to revise our religious services lest we keep alive a form long after the originating spirit of it is dead. It is well also with these men to seek counsel of God before repealing what He has ordained.

5–7. The response is given to *all the people of the land*, and not only to the citizens of Bethel. These men evoked a decision which concerned not only themselves, but the entire Church. The fast *in the seventh month* was held on the third day of the month, the anniversary of the assassination of Gedaliah (Jer. xli. 1–3). *Did ye at all fast unto me, even to me?* or, **Did ye indeed fast unto me?** Why do you come to me, as if I were the gainer or loser by these fasts of yours? It was to serve your own ends you fasted, and it is therefore for you to say whether you should continue to fast. And when ye did eat and when ye did drink, **was it not you who were the eaters, and you who were the drinkers?** It was yourselves you regarded throughout; or, it was only yourselves who benefited either by fasting or feasting. No advantage accrues to God from either the one or the other. Can you not understand that these matters affect only yourselves, and that no such observances are the service I seek? I was not advantaged by your fasting nor by your feasting. It is not by such things you do me service. Why, then, is this the first matter about which you come to consult me? Ought

8 inhabited the south and the plain? And the word of the
9 Lord came unto Zechariah, saying, Thus speaketh the
Lord of hosts, saying, Execute true judgment, and show
10 mercy and compassions every man to his brother: And
oppress not the widow, nor the fatherless, the stranger, nor
the poor; and let none of you imagine evil against his
11 brother in your heart. But they refused to hearken, and
pulled away the shoulder, and stopped their ears, that they
12 should not hear. Yea, they made their hearts *as* an adamant

you not rather to turn your thoughts to the cause of all these sufferings through these seventy years you bewail? ought you not to ask about the words spoken to your fathers, and disregarded by them? *Should ye not hear . . . the former prophets?* or, Is it not the words which the Lord hath cried by the former prophets?—that is to say, Are not these words at the root of this misery of yours? Is not this precisely what these prophets said would follow upon disobedience to their message? Do not get rid of the fasting till you get rid of its root. *The south and the plain,* these together with the "hill country" comprised the territory of Judah (cp. Josh. xv., where this threefold division is used; in ver. 33 the word translated "valley" is the same as that which is here translated "plain." See also Josh. xi. 16; and for the desolation of these parts after the captivity, see Ps. cxxvi. 4).

8. Ewald supposes that this verse crept in by an early clerical error, and certainly the connection between the preceding and succeeding verses is much easier without it. The verse, however, may indicate that the same grand moral laws which had been enjoined upon their fathers was still of primary importance, and that it much more concerned them to know these laws than to hear any response about fast-days.

9, 10. With this republication of those weightier matters of the law, cp. Isa. i. 11-20; Jer. v. 21-23; Micah vi. 6-8; Hos. vi. 6.

11. *Pulled away the shoulder,* like the sulky boy that shakes off the hand that is laid in remonstrance on his shoulder; or like the vicious horse that throws his head in the air when the collar is offered to him; or like the bullock that shies from the yoke (cp. the phrases, *give the cold shoulder, turn the back upon*). For the fact, see Jer. vii. 24, and xi. 7 and 8; Hos. vi. 5, and the actual mission and work of the great series of prophets which was all insufficient to check disloyalty to Jehovah. [Observe the variety of expressions used in the verse, exhibiting persistent, obstinate, stubborn disobedience.]

12. *An adamant stone,* itself used for engraving (the Hebrew word means a sharp-pointed thing, a thorn, a graving tool), and on which nothing could be graven by any other instrument. ἀδάμας, *unconquerable, untameable,* and first used of steel; as in the lines,

"Satan with vast and haughty strides advanc't,
Came tow'ring, arm'd in adamant and gold."

The modern form of the word, "diamond," is also used by Milton in the same sense. "Then Zeal, whose substance is ethereal, arming in complete diamond" (*Apol. for Smect.*). Bacon and Shakespeare use *adamant* to denote the *magnet.*

stone, lest they should hear the law, and the words which the LORD of hosts hath sent in his spirit by the former prophets:
13 therefore came a great wrath from the LORD of hosts. Therefore it is come to pass, *that* as he cried, and they would not hear; so they cried, and I would not hear, saith the LORD of
14 hosts: But I scattered them with a whirlwind among all the nations whom they knew not. Thus the land was desolate after them, that no man passed through nor returned: for they laid the pleasant land desolate.

Hath sent, better, sent. *In his spirit by the former prophets:* lit. in his spirit in the hand of the former prophets, a phrase which clearly and compactly expresses the double agency in prophecy, and the subordinate, instrumental function of the prophets in relation to the Spirit.

13. *Is come,* better, came. Cp. Prov. i. 24–31; Isa. i. 15; Jer. xi. 14; Ps. lxvi. 18, l. 16.

14. *Scattered.* When Mohammed wrote to Chosroes bidding him acknowledge the prophet of God, Chosroes tore the letter in contempt. When Mohammed was informed of this, he said, "Thus will God tear his kingdom and reject his supplications."

REMARKS.—1. It is always a fair, a reasonable, and an advisable question to put regarding any religious observance which has had an incidental origin, whether what was most appropriate a hundred years ago is not mischievous now.

2. There is a self-interested observance of religious ordinances which God cannot acknowledge as having anything to do with Him.

Specify some days set apart for religious service, or some parts of religious worship in Scotland which have had an incidental origin.
Distinguish between a self-interested and a genuine worship.
What is the origin, use, and obligation of fasting? (*Cp. O. and N. T. views of it; also give your opinion regarding Lent, Ramadan, and the fasts of savages to obtain visions.*)
Enumerate the names by which the house of God was known among the Jews.
Learn the Hebrew Calendar; months, fasts, feasts. See *Edersheim's* Temple, 175.
Sherezer. *Mention other heathen names borne by persons or places in Israel. Why were the Quakers wrong in refusing to use such words as Wednesday, Friday, Sunday? Why ought they in consistency to have refused to use the words "disastrous," "ascendancy," "saturnine," "mercurial," "amethyst," "panic," "augury"?*
Stroke the face. *Compare with this the words* "adore," "insinuate," "affront," "insult," and collect similarly-derived words.*

CHAPTER VIII.

1 AGAIN the word of the LORD of hosts came *to me*, saying,
2 Thus saith the LORD of hosts; I was jealous for Zion with great jealousy, and I was jealous for her with great fury.
3 Thus saith the LORD; I am returned unto Zion, and will dwell in the midst of Jerusalem: and Jerusalem shall be called a city of truth; and the mountain of the LORD of hosts
4 the holy mountain. Thus saith the LORD of hosts; There shall yet old men and old women dwell in the streets of Jerusalem, and every man with his staff in his hand for very
5 age. And the streets of the city shall be full of boys and

THE DECISION REGARDING FAST-DAYS—*continued*.

1. *Again*, this word is rather strong; the Hebrew does not suggest any decided break between the two chapters.
2, 3. *I was jealous for Zion*, rather, **I am zealous for Zion.** The Hebrew word is derived from the *redness* of the face which betrays strong emotion (cp. our expressions, "I burn to do so and so," "I blush to think of it"). The strong emotion is felt in favour of Zion; it is not an angry jealousy against Zion that is meant. This is shown in the succeeding clause, which is in the same tense as ver. 2: **I return unto Zion,** *and will dwell in the midst of Jerusalem: and Jerusalem shall be called a city of truth*, etc. These expressions had been rendered familiar by the older prophets as depicting the state of matters resulting from God's inhabitation of Mount Zion.
4. *Dwell*, rather, **sit,** which gives a more graphic picture of the peaceful state indicated. In 1 Macc. xiv. 9 we read that under the government of Simon "the ancient men sat all on the streets, communing together of good things;" long life and abundance of children were reckoned among the blessings of the O. T. "Old age and childhood not only grace a community, the one by its venerableness, the other by its beauty, but they also prove its peace and prosperity" (cp. Bunyan's words, which always call up a picture of peaceful leisure : "But upon a day the good providence of God called me to Bedford, to work at my calling; and in one of the streets of that town I came where there were three or four poor women sitting at a door, in the sun, talking about the things of God," *Grace Abounding*, 37). The existence of old men is the sign that during the past generation no war has been waged.
5. "In the dreadful Irish Famine of 1847, the absence of the children from the streets of Galway was one of its dreariest features. In the dreary back streets and alleys of London the irrepressible joyousness of children is one of the bright sunbeams of that great Babylon" (*Pusey*). Cp. Goldsmith's *Deserted Village:*

"Sweet was the sound, when oft, at evening's close,
Up yonder hill the village murmur rose;
.   .   .   .   .
But now the sounds of population fail,
No cheerful murmurs fluctuate in the gale."

6 girls playing in the streets thereof. Thus saith the LORD of hosts; If it be marvellous in the eyes of the remnant of this people in these days, should it also be marvellous in mine 7 eyes? saith the LORD of hosts. Thus saith the LORD of hosts; Behold, I will save my people from the east country, and from 8 the west country; And I will bring them, and they shall dwell in the midst of Jerusalem: and they shall be my people, and I will be their God, in truth and in righteousness.
9 Thus saith the LORD of hosts; Let your hands be strong, ye that hear in these days these words by the mouth of the prophets, which *were* in the day *that* the foundation of the house of the LORD of hosts was laid, that the temple might 10 be built. For before these days there was no hire for man, nor any hire for beast; neither *was there any* peace to him that went out or came in because of the affliction: for I set 11 all men every one against his neighbour. But now I *will* not *be* unto the residue of this people as in the former days, saith 12 the LORD of hosts. For the seed *shall be* prosperous; the vine shall give her fruit, and the ground shall give her increase, and the heavens shall give their dew; and I will cause the 13 remnant of this people to possess all these *things*. And it

6. Cp. Ps. cxviii. 23, cxxvi. 1, 2.

7. *From the east country, and from the west country, i.e.* from all lands (cp. Matt. viii. 11; Isa. xi. 11 and xliii. 5); lit. **from the land of the rising and from the land of the setting sun.**

9. This and the following verses repeat the argument of Haggai (ii. 15-19). See the notes there. *The prophets, which were in the day*, etc., would almost seem to imply that others besides Haggai and Zechariah had exercised the prophetic function at this time.

10. *No hire for man*, the fields yielded so little that neither man nor beast were remunerated for the toil spent on them. It does not mean that there was no demand for labour, but that labour was unremunerative. Commerce also was difficult and precarious **because of the adversary;** the Samaritans and Ammonites plundering the caravans (cp. Ezra viii. 22). An additional element of distress is added : **and** (not *for*) **I set all men every one against his neighbour.** See the miserable condition described in Neh. v.; and for a somewhat similar state of things, see Carlyle's *French Rev.* i. 178 : "The widow is gathering nettles for her children's dinners; a perfumed Seigneur, delicately lounging in the Œil-de-Bœuf, has an alchemy whereby he will extract from her the third nettle, and name it Rent and Law."

12. *For the seed . . . fruit.* Ewald prefers to translate literally, **But the seed of peace, the vine, shall give her fruit.** The vine is called a *seed* in Ezek. v.; the Hebrew word not covering exactly the same ground as our word *seed;* and the vine is everywhere in the O. T. the symbol of peace and joy. For the latter part of the verse, cp. Hag. i. 10, 11.

13. "The words *curse* and *blessing* are here used, not in the sense of being

shall come to pass, *that* as ye were a curse among the heathen, O house of Judah, and house of Israel; so will I save you, and ye shall be a blessing: fear not, *but* let your hands be
14 strong. For thus saith the LORD of hosts; As I thought to punish you, when your fathers provoked me to wrath, saith
15 the LORD of hosts, and I repented not: So again have I thought in these days to do well unto Jerusalem and to the house of Judah: fear ye not.
16 These *are* the things that ye shall do; Speak ye every man the truth to his neighbour; execute the judgment of truth
17 and peace in your gates: And let none of you imagine evil in your hearts against his neighbour; and love no false oath:
18 for all these *are things* that I hate, saith the LORD. And the
19 word of the LORD of hosts came unto me, saying, Thus saith the LORD of hosts; The fast of the fourth *month*, and the fast of the fifth, and the fast of the seventh, and the fast of the tenth, shall be to the house of Judah joy and gladness, and cheerful feasts; therefore love the truth and peace.
20 Thus saith the LORD of hosts; *It shall* yet *come to pass*, that there shall come people, and the inhabitants of many cities:
21 And the inhabitants of one *city* shall go to another, saying, Let us go speedily to pray before the LORD, and to seek the
22 LORD of hosts: I will go also. Yea, many people and strong nations shall come to seek the LORD of hosts in Jerusalem,

a source of curse and blessing to the heathen, so much as an example of it so striking as to become proverbial" (Moore). Cp. Jer. xxiv. 9: "I will deliver them to be ... a reproach and a proverb, a taunt and a curse ... an astonishment and an hissing." Observe that both the *house of Judah* and the *house of Israel* are addressed. The paragraph closes as it opened with the words, **Be strong.**

14, 15. It is a happy use to make of past sufferings, when men can augur from the fulfilment of God's threatenings that His promises also will be fulfilled (cp. Josh. xxiii. 15).

16-19. The prophet now returns to the direct answer to the question about fasts. He has promised them a prosperous and happy condition in which fasting would be out of place. This condition they are to prolong by righteousness, truthfulness, and loving-kindness. So shall their fasts be turned into feasts. Luther says: "Keep only what I command, and let fasting alone. Yea, if ye keep my commandments, not only shall such fasts cease, but because I will do such good to Jerusalem, all the affliction for which ye have fasted, shall be so forgotten that ye will be transported with joy when ye think of your fasting and your heart's grief which occasioned it." *The fast of the tenth month* commemorated the beginning of the siege of Jerusalem (cp. Jer. xxxix. 1).

20-22. So long as the temple stood, this prediction had but a limited fulfil-

23 and to pray before the LORD. Thus saith the LORD of hosts; In those days *it shall come to pass*, that ten men shall take hold out of all languages of the nations, even shall take hold of the skirt of him that is a Jew, saying, We will go with you: for we have heard *that* God *is* with you.

ment; but the rapid diffusion of the faith which emanated from Jerusalem was the subject of continual remark among writers of the second and third centuries A.D. (cp. *e.g.* Tertullian, *Apol.* 37 : "We are but of yesterday, and we have filled all your places, cities, islands, castles, towns, assemblies, your very camp, tribes, companies, palace, senate, forum").

23. *Ten men, i.e.* a large number. *Ten* expresses totality; when we count up to ten we stop and return to the first unit. This decimal counting was suggested by the number of the fingers. This is proved by the fact that some tribes use their word for *hand* to express the number *five;* and for *ten* they say *both hands;* for *fifteen*, they stretch out both hands and say, *a whole foot;* and for *twenty* they say *one Indian*. For the use of ten as denoting a large number, cp. Gen. xxxi. 7; Neh. iv. 12; Lev. xxvi. 26.

Take hold of the skirt, the natural attitude of one who claims to be listened to or to be protected (cp. 1 Sam. xv. 27; Isa. iv. 1). This prediction has been abundantly fulfilled so far as the western world is concerned. The western world has found its God in Judea. It is God as manifested in the history of the Jews, and especially in the Nazarene, that has been and is acknowledged and worshipped by Christendom. After all the earnest pondering of men, after all the philosophical and scientific investigation by which men in every age have striven to find out God, it is still the skirt of the Jew that forms the most hopeful hold, and gives men the most assured hope of finding Him (cp. John iv. 22, and Rom. xi.).

> *Compare this chapter with the prophecy of Haggai.*
> *Set forth the character of God as exhibited in this chapter.*
> *Compare the teaching about fasts with our Lord's answer to the Pharisees* (Matt. ix. 10–17).
> *To what extent was the prediction of* ver. 23 *fulfilled before Christ came?*
> *What is the meaning, etymologically, of* proselyte, *and what were the laws regarding the proselyte?*
> *Words suggested by this chapter:—Imbecile* (ver. 4), *proletariat* (ver. 5), *heathen* (ver. 13). *What countries derived their names from their position relative to sunrise and sunset?* [*Anatolia, Levant, Hesperia, etc.*, cp. ver. 7.]
> *Explain the use of* gates *in* ver. 16; *give other instances from Scripture of this use; and explain the origin of the custom of judging in the gate.* [*The origin may possibly be found in the nomad custom of pitching the tent of the chief at the extremity of the encampment nearest to the wilderness, so that he might hospitably entertain strangers. He occupied, as it were, the* gate *of the encampment* (cp. Josh. xx. 4, etc.).]
> *What Asiatico-European power derives one of its names from this ancient custom?*

CHAPTER IX.

1 THE burden of the word of the LORD in the land of Hadrach, and Damascus *shall be* the rest thereof: when the eyes of man, as of all the tribes of Israel, *shall be* toward the LORD.
2 And Hamath also shall border thereby; Tyrus, and Zidon,
3 though it be very wise. And Tyrus did build herself a strong hold, and heaped up silver as the dust, and fine gold as the

ISRAEL'S SECURITY AND TRIUMPH AMIDST GENERAL
DISTURBANCE AND DISASTER (ix.–x.).

In these two chapters the prophet depicts a time of great calamity to the cities and territory lying north and south of Israel; but in the midst of this disturbance Judah and Israel shall prosper and see their old foes humbled. The entire section may be divided into four paragraphs, commencing respectively at ix. 1, ix. 9, ix. 16, and x. 8.

1. *Burden*, on this word cp. note on Mal. i. 1. *The land of Hadrach.* In the Assyrian inscriptions it is recorded that "Shalmaneser III. made two expeditions, the first against Damascus in B.C. 773, and the second against Hadrach in B.C. 772; and again that Asshurdanin-il II. made expeditions in B.C. 765 and 755 against Hadrach" (Rawlinson's *Ancient Mon.* iv. 576, quoted in *Speaker's Com.*). Rawlinson is inclined to identify it with Edessa. The expression, *the land of* Hadrach, would seem to indicate that the name was applied to a territory as well as to a town.
Damascus shall be the rest thereof, or, **shall be its resting-place**, not its limit, not the point at which the final blow shall be struck, but merely the place on which the doom predicted shall fall (cp. the very similar expression, Isa. ix. 8, and also Zech. vi. 8). The words, *when the eyes . . . toward the Lord*, should rather be rendered **for Jehovah's eye [supervision] is upon man and upon all Israel's tribes**. This meaning is certified by the concluding clause of the paragraph (ver. 8), and is illustrated by iv. 10. The literal rendering is, **for to Jehovah** [is, or belongs] **the eye of man and of all Israel's tribes**.

2. *And Hamath . . . thereby*, rather **And Hamath also which bordereth thereon**, *i.e.* on the land of Hadrach. Hamath was the principal city of Upper Syria, situated on the Orontes, and commanding the valley of that river (cp. "The entrance of Hamath," Num. xxxiv. 8, and Josh. xiii. 5). Antiochus Epiphanes changed its name to Epiphaneia. It is now called Hamah. The clause, *though* [or, **because**] *it be very wise*, probably refers to Tyre, as the prophets generally refer the fall of Tyre to its over-confidence in its own wisdom. Cp. especially Ezek. xxviii., "Behold, thou art wiser than Daniel . . . with thy wisdom and with thine understanding thou hast gotten thee riches," etc.

3. **Tyre built a tower**, is the nearest approach that can be made in English to the verbal play of the original. *Tyre* is in Hebrew Tzor = *rock*, and *stronghold* is Matzor. The town was considered impregnable, being situated on a rock separated from the mainland by a strait half a mile broad. Curtius

4 mire of the streets. Behold, the Lord will cast her out, and he will smite her power in the sea; and she shall be devoured
5 with fire. Ashkelon shall see *it*, and fear; Gaza also *shall see it*, and be very sorrowful, and Ekron; for her expectation shall be ashamed; and the king shall perish from Gaza, and
6 Ashkelon shall not be inhabited. And a bastard shall dwell in Ashdod, and I will cut off the pride of the Philistines.
7 And I will take away his blood out of his mouth, and his abominations from between his teeth: but he that remaineth, even he, *shall be* for our God, and he shall be as a governor
8 in Judah, and Ekron as a Jebusite. And I will encamp about mine house because of the army, because of him that passeth by, and because of him that returneth: and no oppressor shall pass through them any more: for now have I seen with mine eyes.

(iv. 2) describes the anger of Alexander when the inhabitants refused him the entrance which all the surrounding cities had yielded to him, and how he vowed he would shortly show them that they lived on the mainland. This he did by building the vast mole which to this day makes the site of Tyre appear a promontory rather than an island, and by which he took the city.

4. *Her power in the sea.* The word here translated *power* is in Ezek. xxviii. 5 rendered *riches* (cp. the Latin *opes*, and our *means*). If the words *in the sea* are joined with *power*, then the reference is to merchandise, fleets, harbour, etc.; if they are joined with *smite*, then the meaning is that the treasures of Tyre shall be cast into the sea.

5, 6. The effect of the fall of Tyre on the four chief Philistine cities is described. After taking Tyre, Alexander marched down the coast to Gaza, which also he took after a two months' siege. It was here he was guilty of the enormity of dragging the brave governor Betis round the city in imitation of Achilles. *A bastard shall dwell in Ashdod*, seems equivalent to the prediction of Amos i. 8, "I will cut off the inhabitants from Ashdod;" and might be rendered, **a foreigner shall dwell in Ashdod** (cp. Jer. xlvii., and Zeph. ii. 4, etc.).

7. The Philistines shall be punished for their idolatry. The blood of the sacrifices, which they ate, would be taken out of their mouth (cp. Ps. xvi. 4; Acts xv. 29; Prescott tells us that among the Mexicans the human sacrifices were eaten by the priests and worshippers). At last, this bitterest of Israel's foes will acknowledge Jehovah, and be amalgamated with God's people, so that the governor in Philistia will be, as it were, a governor of part of Judah; and as David once gave the Jebusite a place in Israel (2 Sam. v. 6 and xxiv. 16), so would Ekron now be on a par with this "stranger within the gates" (on the Jebusite, cp. especially Josh. xv. 63).

8. The prophecy of this verse was remarkably fulfilled in the unexpected scathelessness of Jerusalem at the hands of Alexander. Furious as he was at the refusal of the high priest Jaddua to furnish him with supplies while besieging Tyre, and resolved as he was to make an example of Jerusalem, he yet no sooner saw the high priest in his official robes than he recognised him as the

9 Rejoice greatly, O daughter of Zion; shout, O daughter of Jerusalem: behold, thy King cometh unto thee: he *is* just, and having salvation; lowly, and riding upon an ass, and
10 upon a colt the foal of an ass. And I will cut off the chariot from Ephraim, and the horse from Jerusalem, and the battle bow shall be cut off: and he shall speak peace unto the heathen: and his dominion *shall be* from sea *even* to sea, and
11 from the river *even* to the ends of the earth. As for thee also, by the blood of thy covenant I have sent forth thy
12 prisoners out of the pit wherein *is* no water. Turn you to the strong hold, ye prisoners of hope: even to-day do I

same person who had appeared in a dream and promised him victory over the Persians. Accordingly he honoured Jaddua, exempted the Jews from tribute each sabbatical year, and allowed them to live according to their own laws. The story no doubt has been embellished, but the nucleus of fact is remarkable. The cause of all that has been narrated in this and the previous verses is given in the words, *for now have I seen with mine eye.* I have seen that the oppression of my people and the high-handed insolence of the heathen have gone far enough (cp. ver. 1; Ex. ii. 25, iii. 7; and Chaucer, *Man of Law's Tale*, "Our Emperor of Rome, God him see").

9. *Thy King cometh.* Do not quail like the Philistines before this great conqueror, for thy King will come, *just and having salvation*, **righteous and victorious**, *yet lowly*. "In the Messiah the two characteristics which are generally considered incompatible exist in complete harmony; on the one, the divine side, the power both of right and of deed, by which He is always just and never *without help* in need, therefore, is always victorious; on the other, the human side, goodness and gentleness; and He has both together in the fullest measures" (Ewald). He will come *riding upon an ass*, which in the East does not convey any idea of poverty, but only of peace. Had He been a warrior He would have come in His war-chariot or on His war-horse, not on the beast of burden. As King Sapor said to Rabbi Samuel, "You say that the Messiah will come on an ass, I will send Him my splendid charger" (cp. Luke xix. 29).

10. The chariot will be removed from Ephraim, and the horse from Jerusalem, because in this peaceful reign these instruments of war shall no longer be needed. It is not with them that the Messiah extends His conquests and dominion. Yet by His mere word (*He shall speak peace*) will He restore the Davidic kingdom to its largest dimensions, *from sea to sea*, **from the Dead Sea to the Mediterranean** (cp. Ex. xxiii. 31, and especially Ps. lxxii. 8), *and from the river, i.e.* from the Euphrates, *to the ends of the earth.*

11. *By the blood of thy covenant, i.e.* by the blood sprinkled on the people by Moses when Jehovah made a covenant with Israel (Ex. xxiv. 8). It was this which sealed God's promise to be their helper in every such emergency as the present (cp. Ps. cvi. 45, 46). *I have sent forth* is a prophetic perfect equivalent to a future. The purpose is past, and therefore the event is sure. *Thy prisoners* is a figurative expression for all in distress, especially those whose sins had brought distress upon them, as in Ps. cvii. 10-16.

12. The distressed in Israel were *prisoners of hope*, because they had a

13 declare *that* I will render double unto thee; When I have bent Judah for me, filled the bow with Ephraim, and raised up thy sons, O Zion, against thy sons, O Greece, and made
14 thee as the sword of a mighty man. And the LORD shall be seen over them, and his arrow shall go forth as the lightning: and the Lord GOD shall blow the trumpet, and shall
15 go with whirlwinds of the south. The LORD of hosts shall defend them; and they shall devour, and subdue with sling stones; and they shall drink, *and* make a noise as through wine; and they shall be filled like bowls, *and* as the corners of the altar.

prospect of deliverance, a covenant with God. They are summoned therefore to take refuge with God from the threatened calamities of the neighbouring nations, and they shall receive a joy far surpassing their distress (Isa. xl. 2).

13. Judah is represented as the bow, Ephraim as the arrow with which God's enemies are to be subdued; and Zion is the sword, the weapon of the mighty warrior. The reconciliation of this warlike burst with ver. 9, is perhaps best given by comparing it with Isa. xlix. 2 (cp. also Ps. cx. 5; Ps. xlv. 3-5). For the harmonious co-operation of Judah and Ephraim, cp. Isa. xi. 13 with the context; and for the figure, Jer. li. 20, "Thou art my battleaxe and weapons of war."

14. *The Lord shall be seen over them*, as if fighting from heaven in their behalf. Illustrate by the supposed apparition of Castor and Pollux at the battle of Lake Regillus; and of St. James in aid of Cortes and the Spanish troops. The furious onset of the people of God is described in imagery borrowed from the tempests with which the Palestinians were familiar: the rattling of the thunder is the war-trumpet of Jehovah; the swift and fatal lightning, His arrow; and the wild storm blowing from the southern deserts, the resistless fury of His might. So the poet who describes a battle in Italy, draws his imagery of the scattering of the hosts before the Roman onset from Italian scenery:

"So flies the spray of Adria
When the black squall doth blow,
So corn-sheaves in the flood-time
Spin down the whirling Po."

15. In this verse the people are compared to a lion (Num. xxiii. 24) devouring and trampling on the enemy, drinking their blood till he is full of it as the sacrificial bowls, and bespattered with it as the corners of the altar. *Subdue with sling stones*, should rather be, **shall tread upon the sling stones,** *i.e.* no weapon formed against them shall prosper; or, as it is said of leviathan (Job xli. 28), "sling-stones are turned with him into stubble." *Filled like bowls*, the bowls in which the blood of the sacrificial victims was received. The picture is sanguinary, but in keeping with the times (cp. Ps. cxxxvii. 9; Isa. xxx. 27-30). The kindred races in Arabia retained their ferocity to a later period than the Jews. "The 'brave' stamps a red hand upon his mouth to show that he has drunk the blood of the foe. Of the Utaybah 'Harami' it is similarly related that after mortal combat he tastes the dead man's gore" (Burton's *Pilg.* iii. 95). Muir, though thinking the story may be exaggerated, relates (*Life of Mahomet*, iii. 176) that Hind, the wife of Abu Sofian, tore out

16   And the LORD their God shall save them in that day as the flock of his people : for *they shall be as* the stones of a
17 crown, lifted up as an ensign upon his land. For how great *is* his goodness, and how great *is* his beauty ! corn shall make the young men cheerful, and new wine the maids.

the liver of her dead enemy and chewed it, and also strung his nails and pieces of his skin together to bedeck her arms and legs. Of course the stage of society in which such things can actually occur is very different from that in which they survive as figures of speech.

16. With this verse begins a description of the prosperous condition of Israel, commencing with their deliverance and survival of the great day of the Lord's judgment which has been spoken of in the previous paragraph. The *flock* plays an important part in the prophet's imagery from this point onwards. The latter part of this verse is abrupt. Ewald translates, **for crown stones will glitter upon his ground**; and Keil renders, **for stones of a crown are they, sparkling in His land.** It indicates that all God's people would have a kind of regal dignity ; each of them wearing a jewelled head-dress. One would be glad to suppose the words could mean that Jehovah will wear His people as a crown.

17. *How great is his goodness*, *i.e.* how great is the prosperity and beauty of God's people when thus favoured by Jehovah. *Cheerful* might rather be rendered as in the margin, **grow**. As soon as God returns to His people, all dearth, distress, and oppression disappear :

" Now on the place of slaughter
Are cots and sheepfolds seen,
And rows of vines and fields of wheat,
And apple orchards green."

CHAPTER X.

1 ASK ye of the LORD rain in the time of the latter rain ; *so* the LORD shall make bright clouds, and give them showers of

1. *Ask ye of the Lord.* Even in the season in which rain may naturally be expected, Jehovah is to be acknowledged as the sender of it, and prayer is to be made for it. It is not often possible to distinguish between what comes to us in answer to prayer, and what comes to all men or would have come to us in the natural course of events ; but this is no reason for restraining prayer. *Rain*, why rain? Because it is the natural requisite of the agricultural and national prosperity promised in ix. 17 ; and being essential to a country's welfare, it becomes symbolic of all blessing (cp. chap. xiv. 17). *Latter rain.* "The weather . . . became variable with occasional heavy rain, for nearly three weeks longer, until the close of the first week in April. These were the 'latter rains' of Scripture ; which thus continued this season for nearly a month later than usual. One result of these late rains we afterwards saw on our journey, in the very abundant crops of winter grain" (Robinson, *Researches*, iii. 9). *Bright clouds*, rather, **lightnings**, the appropriate accompaniment of **heavy rain, or pouring rain**, as *showers of rain* should be rendered (cp. Jer. x. 13, li. 16 ; Ps. cxxxv. 7).

2 rain, to every one grass in the field. For the idols have
spoken vanity, and the diviners have seen a lie, and have
told false dreams; they comfort in vain: therefore they went
their way as a flock, they were troubled, because *there was* no
3 shepherd. Mine anger was kindled against the shepherds,
and I punished the goats: for the LORD of hosts hath visited
his flock the house of Judah, and hath made them as his
4 goodly horse in the battle. Out of him came forth the corner,
out of him the nail, out of him the battle bow, out of him
5 every oppressor together. And they shall be as mighty *men*,

2. *Idols*, lit. teraphim, little household gods used as oracles. On this and the following clause, see article on "Divination" in Smith's *Dict. of Bible;* and cp. Ezek. xxi. 21, xxii. 28; Jer. xxvii. 9. The great statue of red granite in the Kaaba was brought from Syria to Arabia under the impression that it could give rain. Among all pastoral and agricultural savages, rain-makers hold an influential position. An amusing account of one is given in Baker's *Albert Nyanza*, 252. *Went their way*, lit. shift their tents, or, break up their encampment, as shepherds do when the pasture fails (cp. Jer. l. 6, "They have gone from mountain to hill," etc.).

3. *Punished the goats*. This and the following verbs should be in the future, I will punish. The goats are the powerful who have taken the lead and led badly. The passage which establishes this meaning is Jer. l. 8, "Be as the he-goats before the flocks" (cp. also Isa. xiv. 9). When the flocks of goats go out in the mornings to feed, "the strongest males lead the way over the rocks and chasms, and the whole flock follow in single file" (Van Lennep's *Bible Lands*, i. 202). Neither shepherds nor goats had led the flock to seek blessings from Jehovah, therefore they are to be punished. *Goodly horse*. From being timid and helpless sheep, the people were to become like the war-charger of Jehovah (cp. ix. 13); a figure which not only promises strength and courage to God's people, but reminds them that He Himself advances against the common foe only so far as they carry Him. God does not accomplish His work on earth without the Church, but by means of it.

4. *Out of him, i.e.* from Judah itself, shall her governors and leading men arise. She shall no more be under foreign rule (cp. Jer. xxx. 21). *The corner:* a word commonly used for the chiefs of the people (1 Sam. xiv. 38; Isa. xix. 13), either from the head man being as the corner-stone of a building conspicuous and influential; or from his resembling a mural tower at the corner of a city's ramparts. The passage which connects the Old and New Testament applications of the word is Isa. xxviii. 16. *The nail*. The passage which decides and explains the application of this figure is Isa. xxii. 23, "I will fasten him as a nail in a sure place; and they shall hang upon him all the glory of his father's house," etc. The nail is the man on whom much depends. Nails or pegs are driven into the walls of eastern houses (like those used in harness-rooms with us), and all kinds of utensils, "from the vessels of cups even to the vessels of flagons," are hung upon them. *Every oppressor*. Rather, every ruler or governor. Etymologically the word signifies a driver or taskmaster, one "whose function it is to keep others up to their work."

5. *Tread down . . . battle*, in battle treading them as street mire, an

which tread down *their enemies* in the mire of the streets in the battle: and they shall fight, because the LORD *is* with
6 them, and the riders on horses shall be confounded. And I will strengthen the house of Judah, and I will save the house of Joseph, and I will bring them again to place them; for I have mercy upon them: and they shall be as though I had not cast them off: for I *am* the LORD their God, and will hear
7 them. And *they of* Ephraim shall be like a mighty *man*, and their heart shall rejoice as through wine: yea, their children shall see *it*, and be glad; their heart shall rejoice in the LORD.
8 I will hiss for them, and gather them: for I have redeemed
9 them: and they shall increase as they have increased. And I will sow them among the people: and they shall remember me in far countries; and they shall live with their children,
10 and turn again. I will bring them again also out of the land of Egypt, and gather them out of Assyria; and I will bring them into the land of Gilead and Lebanon; and *place* shall

expression used by David (2 Sam. xxii. 43). The *riders on horses* were especially formidable to Judah, as she was weak in that arm, while it formed the main strength of the great eastern powers. When, *e.g.*, Mahmud the Gaznevide asked a Seljukian chief what cavalry he could supply, he replied, "Send one of my arrows to our camp, and 50,000 men will mount; if these do not suffice, another arrow will summon other 50,000; and if you send my bow through the tribes, the summons will be obeyed by 200,000 horse" (Gibbon, c. 57). Victory over the *riders on horses* was therefore equivalent to complete victory. [Their *confusion* may be illustrated by the panic produced among the Roman cavalry by the elephants of Pyrrhus.]

6. *House of Joseph*, *i.e.* Israel, denoted by its leading tribes, Ephraim and Manasseh, the heirs of Joseph. The promise, *I will bring them again to place them*, might seem to imply that the return from exile had not yet been accomplished. But see Introd. to Zechariah and note on ver. 10.

8. *I will hiss for them*, a common expression in the prophets for the summons which God gives to distant persons. It may either be derived from the noise made to attract bees in hiving, or from the sound naturally made to attract a person's attention. *Them* probably refers to both Judah and Israel. As in Jer. xxx. 20 the return from exile was to be followed by an increase of population, so that their children should be *as aforetime*, so here it is promised that **they shall increase as they increased** of old. The sense is filled up by the next verse, which says:

9. *I will sow them among the people*, that is, **I will not only scatter them among the nations, but give them a prolific root** where they are scattered; an idea still further kept in view by the words, *they shall live with their children*. As Merivale says (*Hist. of the Romans*, xxix.), "the Jews made themselves homes in every country from the Tiber to the Euphrates, from the pines of the Caucasus to the spice-groves of Happy Arabia."

10-12. These verses seem to point not so much to any specific restoration

11 not be found for them. And he shall pass through the sea with affliction, and shall smite the waves in the sea, and all the deeps of the river shall dry up: and the pride of Assyria shall be brought down, and the sceptre of Egypt shall depart 12 away. And I will strengthen them in the LORD; and they shall walk up and down in his name, saith the LORD.

of Jews or Israelites at that time in exile, as to a general reassembling and reorganization of the people of God. On the hypothesis that the promise was given by Zechariah, its suitableness is manifest. Comparatively few of the exiles had returned. The bulk of God's people were still scattered. What was to become of them? Was this not a calamitous weakening of the kingdom of God? Those who have such anxieties are assured that God's people will yet one day live together as a compact community. The assurance is given in the stereotyped language, *I will bring them again out of the land of Egypt, and out of the land of Assyria*, but not on that account was the promise limited to these countries. This is rendered more apparent by the highly poetical language of the next verse, in which the prophet borrows his imagery of the future deliverance and organization of God's people from the normal emancipation, the exodus, the birth-day of the nation. *And he shall pass through the sea with affliction*, or rather, **through the sea of narrowness**, through the sea which presented a narrow threatening passage between the walls of water; *and all the deeps of the river shall dry up*, that is, the fertilizing inundations of the Nile shall be dried up, the source of Egypt's wealth shall fail; and *the sceptre of Egypt*, or, **the rod of the Egyptian taskmaster** which to the Jewish mind still symbolized all bondage, should depart away.

> *Give a summary of what is threatened and promised in these chapters.*
> *Give an account of the fulfilment of* ix. 9; *show distinctly and fully how Christ wins dominion over men, and specify some of the usual methods of establishing kingdoms and gaining influence.*
> *Prayers for rain and for fine weather. Kingsley said: "To pray that there may not be a thunderstorm is to me presumptuous, because the thunderstorm will not come unless it is wanted. To pray that the particular lightning-flash may not strike my child, is not presumptuous." Criticise this.*
> Hadrach *is supposed to be derived from the name of a Syrian god. Give instances of similar derivation.* [Dutch *from Tuisco, the Teutonic Mars;* Mexico *from Mexetla, also the god of war, etc.*]
> Philistine *is probably derived from a word meaning* to migrate, *or to be* a stranger. *What other national names have a similar origin?* [*Vandals, Berbers, Welsh, Wallachians, etc.*] *What does* Palestine *mean?*
> *The pupil should have his attention directed to the similarity of diction between these chapters and the other prophetical books, especially those of Jeremiah and Ezekiel. For this purpose he should be asked to collect parallel passages and expressions.*

CHAPTER XI.

1 OPEN thy doors, O Lebanon, that the fire may devour thy
2 cedars. Howl, fir tree; for the cedar is fallen; because the
mighty are spoiled: howl, O ye oaks of Bashan: for the
3 forest of the vintage is come down. *There is* a voice of the
howling of the shepherds; for their glory is spoiled: a voice

THE GOOD SHEPHERD REJECTED (xi.).

This chapter is a continuation of the prophecy contained in the two preceding chapters; but the character of the prophecy alters: Israel and Judah are now threatened. A note of warning has been given already in x. 3. But that seemed to be launched only against the rulers, and in order that the people might be rescued. Here, however, it becomes obvious that oppression has done its work, hardening and secularizing God's people, so that their restoration and deliverance are fruitless. The prophet therefore now describes the sufferings of God's people under self-seeking rulers, the final opportunity given to them of recognising God's care and submitting themselves to it, and their deliberate rejection of Him as their Shepherd. He then represents God as abandoning the thankless task of tending the flock, and signifying His resolved rejection of them by breaking His crooks, and handing them over to a regardless sham shepherd. It is extremely difficult to establish that this prophecy had any definite preliminary fulfilment previous to the rejection of our Lord, and the consequent ruin of the Jews. Attempts have been made to identify the circumstances here portrayed with those which accompanied the invasion by Tiglath-pileser (2 Kings xv.); but apparently it is rather the first mutter of the far-off Roman conquest that is in the prophet's ear.

1. *Open thy doors, O Lebanon.* The Jews themselves referred this to the destruction of the temple, and they are followed by some modern scholars, who suppose that the temple was so called partly from the cedar which formed so large a part of its material, partly from its prominence and beauty. But apparently it is a violent storm from the north bursting through the Lebanon range, that the prophet describes in these first verses. The lightning splits the tallest cedars; the tempest roars through the forest, the cypresses and oaks crashing and falling before it; the wild beasts are terrified and can find no cover, and the shepherds view with consternation the desolated track of the hurricane. Further definition of this sweeping tempest that bursts through the rocky passes of Lebanon the prophet does not give; what is before his eye, is just what is in his words (cp. the description in Ps. xxix. and in Isa. ii. 10–22).

2. *Fir tree*, rather **cypress.** *Bashan* lies on the northern frontier of Israel to the east of Jordan, as Lebanon formed the frontier to the west of Jordan (cp. x. 10). Bashan has a rich soil, and the hilly district of the north-west portion is clothed with oak forests. *Forest of the vintage* is better rendered as in the margin, **the defenced forest**, or, the **impervious, untrodden forest.**

3. As in Jer. xxv. 34–36, the shepherds are to *howl*, because *their glory, i.e.* their pasture, *is spoiled;* and the lions are to roar, because the tempest has laid

of the roaring of young lions; for the pride of Jordan is spoiled.

4 Thus saith the LORD my God; Feed the flock of the
5 slaughter; Whose possessors slay them, and hold themselves not guilty: and they that sell them say, Blessed *be* the LORD; for I am rich: and their own shepherds pity them
6 not. For I will no more pity the inhabitants of the land, saith the LORD: but, lo, I will deliver the men every one into his neighbour's hand, and into the hand of his king: and they shall smite the land, and out of their hand I will not deliver
7 them. And I will feed the flock of slaughter, *even* you, O

waste *the pride of Jordan*, *i.e.* the thickets or cane-brakes on the banks of Jordan in which the lion made his lair (cp. Jer. xlix. 19 and l. 44, "a lion from the swelling of Jordan").

4. *Thus saith the Lord my God.* Observe the title, and notice that in these three chapters ix., x., and xi., the title "Lord of hosts," so constant in the former part of the book, is rarely, only twice, used. It is to the prophet the words are spoken, and in vision; for the symbolical action which he goes on to represent himself as doing, could only have been done in vision. He could not have fed a flock on the streets of Jerusalem. God's flock is called *the flock of slaughter*, because reared only for slaughter. According to Josephus, the killed in the war under Vespasian numbered 1,356,460, and the prisoners 101,700. During the siege of Jerusalem itself upwards of one million were slaughtered.

5. The chief aggravation of the common woe is that it is brought about by those who should have protected the people. They are a flock *whose possessors slay them*, or, **whose purchasers slaughter them and feel no guilt: and their sellers say, Blessed be Jehovah, I am rich.** God's people were bought and sold. Those who ought to have cherished them handed them over to cruel oppressors. The civil and ecclesiastical governors of Judah and Israel abused their position for their own ends, and their blindness in doing so is exhibited in their saying, "Blessed be Jehovah;" the pious complacency with which men contemplate ill-gotten gain is satirized. The words are strikingly illustrated by the history of the Jews during the century which preceded the fall of Jerusalem (cp. especially Ezek. xxxiv.; Ps. xliv. 11, 12, 22).

6. *For . . . the land.* This gives the fundamental reason for the whole condition of things described in the foregoing verse, and especially for the fact that *their own shepherds pity them not.* They were to be bought and sold and fleeced and slaughtered, because God's pity was no more actively protecting them. They would not submit to God's care, therefore they chose other shepherds who pitied them not. They did not consider themselves well off in God's hand, therefore also *I will deliver the men every one into his neighbour's hand and into the hand of his king.* They shall have an opportunity of testing whether human government is less oppressive than divine government. This verse may well have been remembered and pondered in the days of Herod and the Romans.

7. *I will feed*, rather **I fed**, vers. 7-14 being a description of what the prophet did in compliance with the injunction of ver. 4. The action, as has

poor of the flock. And I took unto me two staves; the one I called Beauty, and the other I called Bands; and I fed the
8 flock. Three shepherds also I cut off in one month; and
9 my soul lothed them, and their soul also abhorred me. Then said I, I will not feed you : that that dieth, let it die ; and that that is to be cut off, let it be cut off ; and let the rest eat
10 every one the flesh of another. And I took my staff, *even* Beauty, and cut it asunder, that I might break my covenant
11 which I had made with all the people. And it was broken in that day : and so the poor of the flock that waited upon

been said, was visionary. Feeding the flock of slaughter, he accordingly fed **the most wretched sheep**; and to do so effectually he took two staves. The shepherds of Asia Minor still carry both " a rod and a staff ; " a short thick cudgel slung at their belt for defence against wild animals, as well as the crook to help the sheep out of holes and marshy ground, or to single out one from the flock, or to guide and keep the flock together. To these he gave significant names (cp. the sword *Excalibur;* Ali's sword *Dhulfekkar;* Thor's hammer *Miölnir,* etc.), calling the one *Beauty,* or rather **Favour,** or **Graciousness** (cp. Ps. xxvii. 4, xc. 17), to keep the other nations from attacking His people ; and the other *Bands* or **Concord,** because with it he would keep the people together as one flock, and preserve them from scattering. The interpretation of the name of the first staff is determined by the tenth verse, which shows that this staff symbolized the protecting care which preserved the people from being destroyed by other nations. God made a covenant with the nations (cp. Hos. ii. 18 ; Job v. 23) to keep them as it were under pledge not to injure His people. The significance of the other staff, as indicating the concord and union of tribe with tribe and class with class, is best illustrated by the striking counterpart of this symbol in Ezek. xxxvii. 15-28.

8. *Three shepherds also I cut off in one month.* Ewald (who assigns the prophecy to the time of Isaiah) says, "We must clearly suppose that King Zechariah, his murderer Shallum, who reigned only a month, and some third ruler, are intended." Wright considers that Antiochus Epiphanes, Antiochus Eupator, and Demetrius are intended by **the three shepherds** ; and that the thirty years between 172 B.C. and 141 B.C. are indicated by the words *in one month,* a prophetic day signifying a year. This suggestion has much to commend it ; but probably that given by Cyril (ii. 458), which supposes that kings, priests, and prophets are meant, best suits the whole context. In this case the expression *one month* must be taken as merely meaning a **short time.** *Lothed them* means **grew impatient,** or **grieved with them,** *i.e.* with the people.

9. Cp. Jer. xv. 1, 2 ; and see Milman's *Hist. of the Jews,* ii. 345, 363, 375.
10. See note on ver. 7. *All the people* should be **all the nations.**
11. *And it was broken, i.e.* the **covenant was dissolved.** *And so . . . Lord,* **And so the wretched sheep which observed me** (the prophet) **knew that it was the word of Jehovah.** Both here and in ver. 7 the expression *the wretched sheep,* or *the poor flock,* applies to the whole of the flock. The prophet saw in his vision that when a sign was given of the covenant being at an end, the people who were giving heed to what he was acting understood that this was God's hand.

12 me knew that it *was* the word of the LORD. And I said unto them, If ye think good, give *me* my price; and if not, forbear.
13 So they weighed for my price thirty *pieces* of silver. And the LORD said unto me, Cast it unto the potter: a goodly price that I was prized at of them. And I took the thirty *pieces* of silver, and cast them to the potter in the house of the LORD.
14 Then I cut asunder mine other staff, *even* Bands, that I might break the brotherhood between Judah and Israel.

12. The prophet personating the shepherd asks for his wages, for his discharge. *So they weighed for my price* [my wages] *thirty pieces of silver*, not because he had served for thirty days (ver. 8), but because this was the sum which the Mosaic law recognised as the just compensation to be given to an owner whose slave had been gored by an ox (Ex. xxi. 32; and cp. Hos. iii. 2). To offer this sum was therefore equivalent to telling the Shepherd of Israel that they could any day buy a common slave who would be as useful to them as He had been. It was either a studied insult, or most probably one of those insults people commit through sheer stupidity and incapacity to understand the persons and things they have to do with. (On weighing money, shekels, etc., see *S. S. Teacher's Bible*, published by Eyre & Spottiswoode.)

13. God pronounces upon the price which the Jews considered a fair equivalent for all the shepherd care that had been spent upon them. **Fling it to the potter, the goodly price** (forsooth) at which I am priced by them. From the circumstance that no piece of ground is so worthless, so much a place for shot rubbish, as a worked-out brickfield or potter's clay-hole, or because pottery was the cheapest of all manufactures and the worst paid at that time, the expression "to the potter with it" may have become a familiar phrase for *throw away the worthless thing*. *A goodly price,* **this magnificent price,** is, of course, ironical—a price you might give for a dish which is produced in thousands, and which will soon find its way to the ashpit with other broken ware; a price you might give for the easiest manufacture—this is the price at which men value the visitation of heaven, the labour of God, the one exceptional thing which throws a light on the world's history, and which nothing can replace. *I took the thirty . . . house of the Lord.* The prophet had not been directed to go to the temple, but he casts the money to the potter there. For what was done in the house of God was done that He might see and remember and take action about it. So this price was to be thrown away contemptuously in the temple as a symbolic expression of the fact that God observed and recorded this ignominy put upon His message and His messenger. (Just as in chap. vi. 14 a memorial in the temple was given to those who acted generously by it.) But the price was probably also cast in the house of the Lord, because the prophet was representing God in his pastoral care, and the wages belonged to God, and were therefore disposed of where all God's dues were paid. After this sum had been offered to God as the price of His care, it was useless making any further offerings; the silver pieces clattering on the temple pavement were the knell of its service. [For the fulfilment of this prophecy, see Matt. xxvii. 9.]

14. "The last winter of Jerusalem passed away in the same ferocious civil contests; her streets ran with the blood of her own children; and instead of

15   And the LORD said unto me, Take unto thee yet the
16 instruments of a foolish shepherd. For, lo, I will raise up a
shepherd in the land, *which* shall not visit those that be cut
off, neither shall seek the young one, nor heal that that is
broken, nor feed that that standeth still: but he shall eat the
17 flesh of the fat, and tear their claws in pieces. Woe to the
idol shepherd that leaveth the flock! the sword *shall be* upon
his arm, and upon his right eye: his arm shall be clean dried
up, and his right eye shall be utterly darkened.

organizing a regular defence against the approaching enemy, each faction was strengthening its own position against the unintermitting assaults of its antagonists. The city was now divided into three distinct garrisons, at fierce and implacable hostility with each other" (Milman, *History of the Jews*, Book xvi. 1). It will be observed that the breaking of the first staff preceded, while the breaking of the second staff succeeded, the final and contemptuous rejection of the Shepherd by the people. This, too, is the historical order. The Jews had long been under foreign rule, Idumæan and Roman, before they were scattered and lost coherence as a nation.

15. The prophet is now directed to personate a foolish shepherd, but it can hardly be supposed that the *instruments* of a foolish shepherd visibly differed from those of a good shepherd. Besides the rod and staff, the eastern shepherd carries in his belt always a knife and often a flute. His provisions he carries in his wallet or "scrip," slung on his back, and he wears a leathern apron (Van Lennep's *Bible Lands*, i. 186-188). The shepherd is not called wicked, but **foolish**. It is the folly of greedy self-seeking that is pointed at. Similarly in Spenser's *Shepherd's Calendar* (July) he describes the "*silie* shepheards*" in terms not very different from those here used:

"Their sheepe have crusts, and they the bread;
The chips, and they the cheese:
They have the fleece, and eke the flesh
(O silly sheepe the while);
The corn is theirs, let others thresh,
Their hands they may not file."

16. Cp. Ezek. xxxiv. 4. *The young one* should be **the scattered**, or strayed. The *tearing of the claws* probably refers to the splitting and cracking of the hoofs by overdriving. When the Good Shepherd was rejected with the words, "We have no king but Cæsar," the Jews chose the foolish shepherd who treated them as this verse describes.

17. *Woe to the idol shepherd*, rather, **Woe, worthless shepherd**. (Cp. Job xiii. 4, "physicians of no value." The word is used of idols as being empty, worthless, "nothing in the world;" but some suppose *idol* is the primary meaning and *worthless* the secondary.)

REMARKS.—1. The thirty pieces of silver unexpectedly emerge in the last scenes of our Lord's connection with the people on whom His shepherd care was spent. (1) This turned out to be the actual sum with which the rulers bought the traitor. When they could no longer stand the Shepherd's interference, and sought to discharge Him, this was the sum they agreed might be given to accomplish this. This was the goodly price at which they and Judas valued Him. (2) This sum was "cast into the house of the Lord." The traitor could not keep it. The coin seemed alive with accusations; it seemed to be turned into so many hissing and stinging serpents; and in the bitterness of his rage against those who had persuaded him to think this paltry sum was of more value than his Master, he hurled the ringing silver at them, as if disannulling the bargain and flinging the guilt back upon them. By so doing he published their disgrace. (3) The sum was actually applied to purchase a worked-out potter's field, worthless for all other purposes, but which was given up for this merely nominal price, and was thought good enough to bury strangers in.

2. As to Matthew's attributing this prophecy to Jeremiah, Luther says: "This and other similar questions do not indeed trouble me very much, because they have but little bearing on the matter; and Matthew does quite enough by quoting a certain Scripture, although he is not quite correct about the name, inasmuch as he quotes prophetic sayings in other places, and yet does not even give the words as they stand in Scripture."

Trace the shepherd symbol through the O. T. to its realization in Christ (Gen. xlix. 24; Ps. lxxvii. 20, lxviii. 70-72, xxiii.).
Give instances of the ill-requitedness of patriots; and specify some of the ways in which we show our estimate of Christ's pastoral care.
"Instead of golden bishops carrying wooden staves, there came to be wooden bishops carrying golden ones"—what period of the Church's history does this refer to? Illustrate the words pastor, crosier, *and the expression* within the pale.
What belief was expressed by the action of the Church described in these lines:

"And then she smiled, and in the Catacombs,
With eye suffused but heart inspirèd true,
On those walls subterranean, where she hid
Her head in ignominy, death, and tombs,
She her Good Shepherd's hasty likeness drew;
And on his shoulders, not a lamb, a kid."

What is the root-meaning of idol; *also of* doll *and* mammet?
Commit to memory lines 108-131 *of Milton's* Lycidas.

CHAPTER XII.

1 THE burden of the word of the LORD for Israel, saith the LORD, which stretcheth forth the heavens, and layeth the foundation of the earth, and formeth the spirit of man within

ISRAEL'S FINAL VICTORY (xii. 1–xiv. 21).

PART I.—Promise is given to Jerusalem and Judah of dearly-bought victory, a gracious mourning, and zealous reformation (xii. 1–xiii. 6).
α. Jerusalem besieged and delivered (xii. 1-9).
β. The national mourning (xii. 10-14).
γ. The cleansing of the nation (xiii. 1-6).

2 him. **Behold, I will make Jerusalem a cup of trembling unto all the people round about, when they shall be in the siege**

It is obvious that from the beginning of the twelfth chapter to the end of the book it is one period that is described. This is indicated especially by the actual contents of the prophecy, but also by the continuous use of the phrase "in that day," and by the fact that while a fresh heading is given in chap. xii. 1 no further heading occurs. But the prophet does not appear to proceed through these chapters as if he were carefully adhering to a chronologically continuous view of events, but rather as if his mind were recalled by their magnitude to depict the same events from another point of view. It is not a slowly evolving panorama of one continuous landscape that passes before the eye, but two views of the same scene looked at from different points. The first of these views is contained in chap. xii. 1-xiii. 6. In this passage the prophet describes a time in the highest degree critical for Jerusalem, but which by Jehovah's interference will result in victory to His people. But accompanying this promise of victory there is none of the usual enlargement regarding material prosperity, but a very striking and abrupt announcement of certain moral and spiritual benefits which were to result from this conflict. We look in vain for any historical occurrences in which the letter of this prophecy has been fulfilled to Israel after the flesh, unless it be in the Maccabean period. What the prophet sees is the vanity of all attempts to extinguish God's people, the penitent return of that people to the king they had rejected, and the consequent zeal in putting away those who had misled them.

1. *The burden*, see on Mal. i. 1. *For Israel*, or, **concerning Israel**. Yet it is Judah that is spoken of. Bleek thinks this an evidence of the pre-exilian authorship of this prophecy, arguing that only in the few years preceding the captivity was Judah the sole representative of Israel in the Holy Land. But it may with equal justice be argued that only in post-exilian times did Judah begin to be used as a general term including all Israel, while yet *Israel* retained its significance as a religious designation (cp. Ezra ix. 1, 4, 15, x. 1, 9, 10). The *word* is from **Jehovah**, *which stretcheth . . . within him*, or rather, **who spread forth the heavens, and founded the earth, and formed man's spirit within him**—that is, from Him who has power to bring to pass what He promises (cp. Isa. xlii. 5; Amos iv. 13); and this, even where man's free-will is an element determining events.

2. *Behold . . . round about*, or, **Behold, I make Jerusalem a bowl of reeling for all the peoples around**. The assaults made on Jerusalem by those who thirst for her spoil shall be hurtful to themselves. The cup they eagerly drink shall confuse and bewilder them. The figure is common in the prophets. See Ps. lxxv. 8; Jer. li. 7; Isa. li. 17; Ps. lx. 3; and "The earth shall reel to and fro like a drunkard," Isa. xxiv. 20. About the meaning of the second clause there is great diversity of opinion. Literally rendered, the words are, **and also against Judah shall it be in the siege against Jerusalem**, which would seem to indicate that Judah would participate with Jerusalem in the anxiety and suffering produced by the invading army. [It is just possible that the preposition should be translated **concerning**, which would thus make Judah as well as Israel the object of the *burden* proclaimed in the first verse. In either case the clause seems to be slightly out of the place we should expect it in.]

3 both against Judah *and* against Jerusalem. And in that day will I make Jerusalem a burdensome stone for all people: all that burden themselves with it shall be cut in pieces, though all the people of the earth be gathered together
4 against it. In that day, saith the LORD, I will smite every horse with astonishment, and his rider with madness: and I will open mine eyes upon the house of Judah, and will smite
5 every horse of the people with blindness. And the governors of Judah shall say in their heart, The inhabitants of Jerusalem
6 *shall be* my strength in the LORD of hosts their God. In that day will I make the governors of Judah like an hearth of fire among the wood, and like a torch of fire in a sheaf; and they shall devour all the people round about, on the right hand and on the left: and Jerusalem shall be inhabited again in

3. *A burdensome stone.* Those who seek to carry off the spoil, or who take the management of the city, or who desire in any way to use it for their own purposes, will find it a crushing weight. But whence the figure? Is it, as Jerome supposes, from the custom among villagers and athletes of testing strength by lifting heavy stones, in accordance with which Ewald translates it *a lifting stone*, or, as we should say, *a putting stone?* Far more probably there is no such reference, but a mere general allusion to a weight that is too heavy to be borne; as Henry Taylor says in another connection: "Thinking to hang a trinket round their neck, they find it a millstone." Taking in hand to form the destiny of Jerusalem, they find it a crushing task. "May it please your Majesty," said Rivet, "the Church is an anvil that hath broken a great many hammers" (Lange). Note the striking coincidence and difference between the figures used here and in Isa. xxiv. 20.

4. Cp. Deut. xxviii. 28 with Deut. xxx. 7. "The Lord shall smite thee with madness and blindness and astonishment of heart." See also 2 Kings vi. 18. *I will open mine eyes.* The eyes of Jehovah will be upon His people to protect them : the eyes of the enemy shall be blinded (cp. note on x. 5).

5, 6. *The governors of Judah*, **the chief men, the heads of families.** [The Hebrew word is not often applied to *Jewish* leaders. It is derived from the same root as *Aleph*, the first letter in the Hebrew *Alpha*bet. This is one of the roots which shows capacity for ramification. Its radical meaning is *to be familiar with, to be associated with*, and so there is derived from it Aleph, *an ox*, man's *associate, the* domestic animal; and Aleph, *a thousand*, and also *a family*, the idea in both cases being *an association*, a company banded together.] This verse begins to call attention to the two elements in the Jewish community; the dwellers in Judah, and the inhabitants of Jerusalem. It predicts their complete harmony and mutual reliance and helpfulness, although there are signs (ver. 7) of a natural disposition in the metropolitans to despise the provincials and take to themselves an undue share of credit. It is difficult to fix on any period of Jewish history which was characterized by this marked distinction between town and country; or by the circumstance emphasized in ver. 6, that Jerusalem was defended and delivered by those outside her walls. Other two features of the time are alluded to: that the enemy should vastly outnumber the home troops, but should only thereby be

7 her own place, *even* in Jerusalem. The LORD also shall save the tents of Judah first, that the glory of the house of David and the glory of the inhabitants of Jerusalem do not magnify
8 *themselves* against Judah. In that day shall the LORD defend the inhabitants of Jerusalem; and he that is feeble among them at that day shall be as David; and the house of David
9 *shall be* as God, as the angel of the LORD before them. And it shall come to pass in that day, *that* I will seek to destroy
10 all the nations that come against Jerusalem. And I will pour upon the house of David, and upon the inhabitants of Jerusalem, the spirit of grace and of supplications: and they shall look upon me whom they have pierced, and they shall mourn for him, as one mourneth for *his* only *son*, and shall be in bitterness for him, as one that is in bitterness for *his*

as more abundant fuel to their warlike rage (**like a brazier, or pan of fire, among faggots, or like a torch overlaid with corn**, making thereby only the fiercer blaze); and that **Jerusalem should be again inhabited**. The first and the third feature are found in the time of Nehemiah (chap. xi.); but in his time, although the enemies of the Jews were certainly active, they were not so formidable as this prophecy would imply. So that some may be disposed to find the fulfilment rather in the Maccabean period, when the enemy was certainly sufficiently formidable and vastly superior in numbers to the gallant bands that maintained the Jewish independence. Jerusalem was taken by Ptolemy, one of Alexander's successors, in B.C. 321, when 100,000 captives were deported to Alexandria and Cyrene; and again by Antiochus Epiphanes in B.C. 167, when 40,000 of the inhabitants were massacred, as many sold, and the temple pillaged and desecrated; so that when Judas, the Maccabee, gained possession of the city, he found it desolate, and the temple-courts overgrown with brushwood.

7. This verse also rather points to the Maccabean period, as Judas, beginning his career of conquest from Modin, a town on the road between Jerusalem and Joppa, drove the Syrians from the country round Jerusalem before he relieved the city itself.

8. *Shall the Lord defend.* Read the prayer of Judas, 1 Macc. iv. *He that is feeble,* **the tottering one**. One illustration of this may be found in Mattathias, the father of the five Maccabees, who, though an old man, struck the first blow for the recovery of Jewish liberties. In general it is an encouragement to believe that in the day of need the weaklings of the future shall equal the heroes of the past; and the strong shall resemble the angel that led the host of Israel when the Egyptians and all Israel's enemies were consumed (Ex. xxiii. 20; Josh. v. 13).

10-14. *The spirit of grace and of supplications* (cp. Joel ii. 28; Ezek. xxxix. 29). Ewald translates, **a spirit of love and love-seeking**; both words are from the same root, and would therefore naturally signify two branches or manifestations of the same root-grace communicated by God. But the former of the two words is commonly and rightly rendered *favour* or *grace*, and if used in this sense here it must refer to a new disposition towards God springing up in the people, **a spirit of relenting, of contrition for rejecting**

11 first-born. In that day shall there be a great mourning in Jerusalem, as the mourning of Hadadrimmon in the valley of
12 Megiddon. And the land shall mourn, every family apart; the family of the house of David apart, and their wives apart; the family of the house of Nathan apart, and their wives
13 apart; The family of the house of Levi apart, and their wives
14 apart; the family of Shimei apart, and their wives apart; All the families that remain, every family apart, and their wives apart.

God, of **willingness to accept Him**, in a word, of love, but of love that has in it the element of tender compunction about its past treatment of God. The second word refers rather to the **expressions of love**, the trustful cries for help and acknowledgments of dependence which accompany this relenting. But what is the meaning of the mourning which the prophet declares shall be the immediate result of this new spiritual life, *they shall look upon me whom they have pierced?* There seems to be no doubt that the reading is correct, though Ewald and others evade the difficulty by inserting a letter, and reading **they shall look upon him**, that is, upon some unknown martyr in the cause of Jerusalem. *Upon me* must mean either **upon me, Jehovah**, in which case the word *pierced* must be taken, as Calvin takes it, in a figurative sense (as we speak of *wounding* one's feelings, or *cutting* the heart); or, **upon me, the prophet**, who was the speaker of these words and the representative of Jehovah. So Hitzig: "The passage may most easily be explained from the identification of the Sender with the Sent, of Jehovah with the prophet." Calvin's mode of interpretation seems preferable. Those who first heard the words must have disconnected the **me** of the one clause from the **him** of the other, and thought of some figurative *piercing* of Jehovah, that is, of some rebellious, fiercely insolent treatment of Jehovah, displayed and expressed especially in the death of some person who represented Jehovah and His cause. They wake up to the perception that by their abusive treatment of some one who has been slain by them, they have *pierced* Jehovah. A closer identification of the *me* and the *him*, of Jehovah and His martyr, is inconsistent with the O. T. view of Jehovah and His modes of manifestation, and it is only in Christ that the identification becomes perfect, and the prophecy fully satisfied. This is borne out by the comparison instituted between the mourning here spoken of and the mourning for Josiah. At least it seems something more than a coincidence that the much-loved Josiah met his death in a cause that was not strictly his own, in a battle from which his enemy himself warned him away as from a quarrel with which he had nothing to do (2 Chron. xxxv. 21). Josiah's sense of honour, as king of Judah, prevented him from listening to this warning; he went to battle and was pierced to his death. And as the people saw him slowly driven into Jerusalem, his life's blood dripping from his chariot, their mourning was tenfold more bitter because they knew it was not in any private quarrel of his own he had fallen, but that he had died as their king, sacrificed to his position as ruler of a people involved in many hereditary quarrels and difficulties. The mourning was national, like this predicted mourning—*the land shall mourn, every family apart.* Every family felt the bereavement. The man whose private prosperity prevented him from shedding a tear over the fallen king would have been justly denounced as a heartless traitor. The man who could not understand what the people meant by crying in the streets "we have pierced our king," might well have been denounced as incredibly selfish, the worst kind of citizen. (Illustrate by the mourning after Flodden, when "the Flowers of the Forest were a' wede away;" or by the national sorrow at the death of Louis XII. of France, when the criers went through the streets, crying, "The good King Louis, father of the people, is dead;" or by the profound gloom which settled upon Paris when Mirabeau expired, of which Carlyle says, "For three days there is low wide moan; all theatres, public amusements close; the people break in upon private dancing parties, and sullenly command that they cease. . . . In the Restaurateur's at the Palais-Royal, the waiter remarks, 'Fine weather, Monsieur;' 'Yes, my friend,' answers the ancient man of letters, 'very fine; but Mirabeau is dead;'" but especially by the lamentation for Judas Maccabaeus, when "all Israel bewailed and lamented him with a sore lamentation, and mourned for many days, and said, 'How is he fallen that was mighty to save Israel,'" 1 Macc. ix. 20.)

This mourning for Josiah is here spoken of as *the mourning of Hadadrimmon in the valley of Megiddon.* Jerome says: "Hadadrimmon is a city near Jerusalem, now called Maximianopolis, in the field of Mageddon, where the good king Josiah was wounded by Pharaoh-Necho." Assyrian scholars have shown that the correct form of the word is **Hadar-Ramman**; that it means **Glorious is the Exalted One**, or **Glorious is Ramman**, Ramman being the Assyrian Storm-god; and that the name was probably given to the town by Assyrian colonists. (Observe the bearing of this on the date of the prophecy. It is *possible* the name may have been given to the town earlier than the captivity, but surely the probability is that the name was given by Assyrian settlers after the land was taken from the Jewish inhabitants.) Attention is directed to the reality and depth of the national mourning by the expression *every family apart;* it was not an officially-ordered mourning, a court-mourning for so many days, but a genuine sorrow visible as much in the family circle as in public. In Christian contrition alone does this feature find adequate fulfilment, although in Christian contrition the *national* character of the mourning is not exhibited. "In countless numbers of retired chambers, the sighs and prayers of individuals have ascended to heaven" (Pressel). As instances, four families are named, the two leading and the two subordinate families of the royal and priestly lines, *Nathan* representing a branch of David's house (2 Sam. v. 14), and *Shimei* representing a branch of Levi's house (Ex. vi. 17). See Questions.

CHAPTER XIII.

1 In that day there shall be a fountain opened to the house of David and to the inhabitants of Jerusalem for sin and for

1. *A fountain opened . . . for sin and for uncleanness.* The Jewish mind was familiar with the idea of *washing* from sin and from ceremonial impurity (cp. the washings enjoined by the law, and also Ezek. xxxvi. 25 : "Then will I sprinkle clean water upon you, and ye shall be clean; from all your filthi-

2 uncleanness. And it shall come to pass in that day, saith the LORD of hosts, *that* I will cut off the names of the idols out of the land, and they shall no more be remembered: and also I will cause the prophets and the unclean spirit to
3 pass out of the land. And it shall come to pass, *that* when any shall yet prophesy, then his father and his mother that begat him shall say unto him, Thou shalt not live; for thou speakest lies in the name of the LORD: and his father and his mother that begat him shall thrust him through when he
4 prophesieth. And it shall come to pass in that day, *that* the prophets shall be ashamed every one of his vision, when he hath prophesied; neither shall they wear a rough garment to

ness and from all your idols, will I cleanse you"). For the significance, see notes on chap. iii.; and illustrate the thoroughness of God's forgiveness and cleansing by the result of washing in water; which is, that the same stains can never again appear, though similar ones may. The identical filth cannot be gathered out of the water and be replaced on our hands; the stains, the sins, are, as we say, "*clean* gone," gone quite away. The prophet's contemporaries would accept this as figurative language implying their acceptance with God, forgiveness, and renewal.

2. *Idols.* Idolatry was not so rife in Israel after as before the captivity. But in a prophecy dealing so much in general language as this does, it seems quite admissible to suppose that the prophet here, as elsewhere, speaks of things future under the well-known forms of the past, and in idolatry and false prophecy sees ungodliness in general. Moreover, if the prophecy does refer to the Maccabean period, then nothing could be more in point than this promise to cleanse the land from idols. The adoption of Greek customs and worship was the temptation of that period. And so subtly prevalent was idolatry, that little idols were found in the clothes of some even of the priests who had fallen in battle *against* the Greeks (cp. also Ezra ix. 1). By the *unclean spirit* is probably meant the inward disposition which led men to the *sin* (not the *uncleanness,* for that has a different meaning) for which the fountain was opened. There may be a contrast intended between *the spirit of penitence* spoken of in ver. 10 above, and this *unclean spirit* (cp. also 1 Kings xxii. 22).

3. The zeal of the contrite nation against false prophecy is represented by its most striking instance. Parents would slay their own son, their one hope, the promising lad in whose future they lived, if they saw in him a leaning to the sins which had blighted their land (cp. Deut. xiii. 1-11, xviii. 20). So afraid were they of being again betrayed into the awful iniquity of **thrusting through** Jehovah in His true representative, that rather than admit such a possibility they would **thrust through** their own child.

4-6. The Jewish public shall be so alive to the danger of being misled that false prophecy shall become a very perilous and uninviting vocation. If any one continues to exercise such a function, he will do it secretly: he shall not *wear a rough garment to deceive,* he will not attempt to gain credence for his words by assuming the prophet's professional garb. This garb was either an untanned sheepskin, or a cloak, like the Bedouin blanket, made of camel's hair, as the Baptist's was. The false prophets are the progenitors of the

5 deceive: But he shall say, I *am* no prophet, I *am* an husbandman; for man taught me to keep cattle from my
6 youth. And *one* shall say unto him, What *are* these wounds in thine hands? Then he shall answer, *Those* with which I was wounded *in* the house of my friends.

modern begging dervishes, and these dervishes are distinguished by wearing a single sheepskin over their shoulders and no other covering save a leather girdle round their loins. (For a very interesting account of a more respectable prophet, see Livingstone's *Missionary Travels*, p. 87; and illustrate the verse by the fact that when Domitian banished philosophers from Rome, many persons shaved off their beards, and flung away their cloaks, that they might not be included in the ban.) Far from attempting to attract attention, the false prophet will deny his vocation if challenged regarding it. *I am no prophet, I am an husbandman.* I belong to that class in society which lies under the least suspicion of aspiring to a function in which knowledge of affairs, dexterity in making use of men's weaknesses, and some literary faculty are needed. Besides, **men own me (use me as a slave) from my youth** (for this is the meaning of the words rendered, *for man taught me to keep cattle from my youth*), and so if I had had the will I could never have had the chance of setting up as a prophet. I have not been my own master. Not quite satisfied with this disclaimer, the supposed examiners ask to be allowed to look at his hands, as you can judge roughly of a man's calling by the state of his hands, at least you can thus judge whether a man is earning his bread with his hands or with his head. They at once detect suspicious marks on this man's hands, wounds which they evidently suspect to have been self-inflicted in accordance with some idolatrous rite. Self-mutilation and self-laceration have always been common accessories of pagan worship, and common accompaniments and manifestations of pagan fanatical ecstasy. They are far from uncommon still in heathen, and even in Mohammedan countries. Permanent marks of a distinctive kind were also frequently made upon different parts of the person, and especially upon the arms, in acknowledgment of allegiance to some particular god (cp. Jer. xlviii. 37, where mourning is described thus: "Every head shall be bald, and every beard clipped: *upon all the hands* shall be cuttings"). But the man denies that his wounds have any such significance; they are not, he says, religious marks at all: they are wounds which I received *in the house of my friends*, in some rustic frolic with his boon-companions, or as the slave's brand in the house of his master. [It is no doubt possible to construe this as an admission of the charge against him, and as conveying the meaning that his friends, his parents (cp. ver. 3), had punished him for false prophesying. But this interpretation seems less consistent and natural.] To apply such an allusion to our Lord from the mere circumstance of a mention of *wounds in the hands* is a careless and superficial mode of dealing with the O. T. which cannot be too strongly reprehended. Were it adopted by an adversary of the faith, one would suppose it to be profanity.

REMARKS.—This is one of the prophecies which seem to point to a *national* repentance on the part of the Jews. Such a national, simultaneous, obvious mourning as these words indicate can be exhibited only by that one nation which crucified their long-expected King. And nothing would go further toward the conversion of the world than were the Jews to complete their

7 Awake, O sword, against my shepherd, and against the man *that is* my fellow, saith the LORD of hosts: smite the marvellous history by once again combining, and this time to acknowledge Jesus as the Christ, their and the world's King. The agony of remorse would be terrible. But what event could be so exemplary to the world? Who could be such missionaries as those from whom the apostles sprang, and who are now found in every nation, and speaking every language of the world?

The zeal of the reformed nation (chap. xiii.). In the detection of the same old evil, although the old dress had been thrown aside, in the detection of the characteristic marks even when much in the outward form was altered, we see the keenness of a pure and righteous intention which means that war with sin shall be war to the knife, a war of extermination.

> *Give reasons for and against supposing that this prophecy warrants the expectation that the Jews as a nation will return to the Lord. What would be the probable consequences of such a national submission to Christ?*
> *Explain how the prediction of ver. 10 is fulfilled in Christ.*
> *Give instances which exemplify the mourning of the house of David; also of the house of Levi, for the death of Christ.*
> *Explain Paul's belief regarding the national repentance of the Jews; 'and what he means by the words: "If the casting away of them be the reconciling of the world, what shall the receiving of them be but life from the dead?"*
> *Illustrate, from the reforming zeal of Israel, the following lines:*
>> " For what is true repentance, but in thought,
>> Not even in inmost thought, to think again
>> The sins that made the past so pleasant to us?"
>
> *When God revives His people, He gives repentance, cleansing, and zeal: men feel a humble compunction for Christ's death, they long for pardon and inward purity, and they relentlessly exterminate their own evil habits.*

ISRAEL'S FINAL VICTORY (xii. 1–xiv. 21).

PART II.—The Day of the Lord (xiii. 7–xiv. 21).
This closing prophecy seems less a chronological continuation of the preceding than a closer, more penetrating, and far-reaching view of the results of those ruling principles whose operation was to some extent described in the former. It is as if a skilled physician, studying the constitutional weaknesses and probable environment of a child, were to describe the course his illnesses would take; depicting first one attack and then another, and showing how the same causes would produce increasingly serious results. The highly figurative representation here given cannot be taken as if it were a realistic picture of some one event. It is intended to show the working of certain principles, and to convey the impression that God's people will triumph, but only by their passing through most critical times, and by His miraculous and *personal* interposition. It shows us the day of the Lord opening in gloom, but light at evening, when it promised to be darkest; great calamities falling on the city of God, but resulting in her being lifted up as the conspicuous, life-giving metropolis of the race.

7. *Awake, O sword.* This abrupt cry indicates that a fresh beginning is

shepherd, and the sheep shall be scattered: and I will turn
8 mine hand upon the little ones. And it shall come to pass,
that in all the land, saith the LORD, two parts therein shall
be cut off *and* die; but the third shall be left therein.
9 And I will bring the third part through the fire, and will
refine them as silver is refined, and will try them as gold is
tried: they shall call on my name, and I will hear them: I
will say, It *is* my people: and they shall say, The LORD *is*
my God.

made. Yet there is much to be said in favour of the view that this summons to the sword is suggested by the religious declension which followed the religious zeal described in the foregoing verses as characterizing the Maccabean period. The following words should be pondered: "One unclean spirit departed (cp. ver. 3), but seven unclean spirits took its place. In place of superstition there sprang up irreligion. Bigotry took the place of righteous zeal. The sword of judgment, which in a theocracy might justly have been unsheathed against the impostor, was drawn to smite the true prophet of God" (Wright's *Bampton Lect.* p. 437). For the expression, cp. Ps. xliv. 23, "Awake, why sleepest thou, O Lord?" and Jer. xlvii. 6, where the sword is appealed to, to sheathe itself and be at rest. *My shepherd* might be applied to any ruler of God's people, as *e.g.* to Cyrus (Isa. xliv. 28). The person meant is further defined by the words, *the man that is my fellow*, lit. **a man my fellow**, so designated from his having a fellowship of interest with Jehovah, both working towards one end and by the same means. The word means a **fellow-tribesman** or **fellow-citizen**, that is, one whose interests are the same, and who may be of the same blood. To the Jewish ear previous to the Incarnation, it could only convey the former idea, the idea of a person closely allied to God by community of interest. The Incarnation fills the words with the meaning which the Spirit of God designed they should carry. *Smite the shepherd, and the sheep shall be scattered* (cp. 1 Kings xxii. 17). Because the sheep refuse the shepherd's care, and cannot be convinced of the benefit of it till they feel the want of it, the shepherd must be slain (for *smiting with the sword* means **slaying**), that they may be reclaimed to God's pastoral care. The *scattering* is the first effect; but *I will turn mine hand* (for good, cp. Isa. i. 25) *upon the little ones*, or rather upon those who appear little, **the humble**, those who long to be able to say, "Jehovah is my Shepherd." The idea of slaying the shepherd, though faithful and doing his work well, for the sheep's sake, had been already rendered familiar by the similar prediction regarding the Servant of Jehovah in Isa. liii. Cp. the application of this prophecy to Himself by our Lord the night of His betrayal, Matt. xxvi. 31.

8. *The third* is, of course, not intended to express the exact proportion, but only to signify in a general way that a comparatively small number would be saved.

CHAPTER XIV.

1 BEHOLD, the day of the LORD cometh, and thy spoil shall be
2 divided in the midst of thee. For I will gather all nations against Jerusalem to battle; and the city shall be taken, and the houses rifled, and the women ravished; and half of the city shall go forth into captivity, and the residue of the
3 people shall not be cut off from the city. Then shall the LORD go forth, and fight against those nations, as when he
4 fought in the day of battle. And his feet shall stand in that day upon the mount of Olives, which *is* before Jerusalem on the east, and the mount of Olives shall cleave in the midst thereof toward the east and toward the west, *and there shall be* a very great valley; and half of the mountain shall remove
5 toward the north, and half of it toward the south. And ye

1-5. *The day of the Lord cometh*, lit. **a day cometh for Jehovah**, a day belonging in a special way to Him, as giving opportunity for the rapid development or consummation of His purposes. The first striking mark of this day is in this, that Jerusalem's extremity had come. *Thy spoil shall be divided in the midst of thee*, etc. Already the enemies of Jerusalem have stormed the city and are sacking it; she is suffering all the horrors which even well-disciplined troops can scarcely be withheld from inflicting on a town that has long resisted their siege; heaps of spoil are piled up in her open squares, and savage soldiers are quarrelling over the booty; the women and children and men who have escaped the first slaughter are tremblingly awaiting their fate—at this juncture a new champion appears. *Then shall the Lord go forth*, not now merely in the persons of those commanders to whom His authority has been delegated, but *His feet shall stand upon the Mount of Olives*. In some awful personal manifestation such as that which shook Sinai, shall He appear, and *the Mount of Olives shall cleave*, the line of cleavage running east and west, and cutting so deep as to form a ravine. (For the appearance of the Lord with earthquake, cp. Isa. xxix. 6; Ezek. xxxviii. 19, 20: and for the other accompaniment, *all the saints with thee*, Deut. xxxiii. 2; also Joel iii. 11.) It is commonly understood that this ravine is provided for the escape of God's people through the Mount of Olives, but escape was now unnecessary. The presence of Jehovah was the discomfiture of their foes. Besides, their present flight is compared to the flight of those who *fled from before the earthquake in the days of Uzziah*. People fled then panic-stricken, and fled from the spots where the presence of the earthquake was displayed. So now they shall flee *from* the earthquake and in terror, precisely as they had done at Sinai also, and as men always do at a near manifestation of God. The reason given also shows that this is meant, *for the valley of the mountains shall reach unto Azal*, or, as it should rather be translated, **for the valley of the mountains shall reach to very near you**, it shall be alarmingly close. The panic will, of course, be short-lived, like the panic of those who are hard pressed in battle, and fancy that the flashing of weapons through the dust and shall flee *to* the valley of the mountains; for the valley of the mountains shall reach unto Azal: yea, ye shall flee, like as ye fled from before the earthquake in the days of Uzziah king of Judah: and the LORD my God shall come, *and* all the saints 6 with thee. And it shall come to pass in that day, *that* the 7 light shall not be clear, *nor* dark: But it shall be one day which shall be known to the LORD, not day, nor night: but it shall come to pass, *that* at evening time it shall be light.

smoke on their flank denotes the approach of fresh enemies, but find that they are friends. *The earthquake in the days of Uzziah* is not mentioned in the history, but it was so memorable an event in the popular mind as to form an era from which other events were dated (see Amos i. 1, and cp. "two years after Waterloo," etc. In Crete all recent events are dated by such eras as "the year of the great earthquake, the outbreak of the Greek revolution," etc., Blakesley's *Herodotus*, i. 263). Josephus, who connects the earthquake with the sin of Uzziah, gives a highly-coloured description of its violence (*Ant.* ix. 10. 4). In Plumptre's elegant and suggestive *Biblical Studies*, ten pages well worth consulting are devoted to this subject. Cp. Isa. ii. 10–22, xxiv. 18–20.

6-11. Further description of this notable day, and the deliverance it will bring to Jerusalem. *The light shall not be clear nor dark*, rather, there shall be no light, shining ones [*i.e.* the stars, and possibly also the sun and moon] shall be withdrawn, in accordance with the consenting utterances of the other prophets who describe the day of the Lord; as Joel (ii. 31), "The sun shall be turned into darkness, and the moon into blood;" and again (iii. 15), in a passage remarkably parallel to this, "The sun and the moon shall be darkened, and the stars shall withdraw their shining." Cp. also Ezek. xxxii. 7; Zeph. i. 15; as well as Matt. xxiv. 29; Rev. vi. 12, 13. It is to be a day of portentous gloom, such as Milton describes:

"The morn
In dim eclipse disastrous twilight shed."

7. *But it shall be one day*, or, as we should say, it will be unique and by itself, the only one of its kind; as Jeremiah (xxx. 7) says: "Alas! for that day is great, so that none is like it." Here it seems to be its obscure light which gives it this peculiar character; it is to be *not day, nor night*, but a kind of murky twilight, all the more alarming in countries where twilight and mist are unknown, where

"The sun's rim dips, the stars rush out,
At one stride comes the dark."

Like the awful gloom that accompanies a sand-storm, terrifying man and beast, would be the portentous obscurity of this unique day. But though resembling no other day, *it is known to the Lord*. "True, that is a day such as no man has yet seen; but Jehovah knows it, with Him it is possible, and He will cause it to come" (Ewald). And though the day opens in gloom, yet *at evening time*—when the dimness is expected to deepen into pitch darkness—*it shall be light*. The period which has been marked by unprecedented calamities shall clear and brighten towards its close.

8 And it shall be in that day, *that* living waters shall go out from Jerusalem; half of them toward the former sea, and half of them toward the hinder sea: in summer and in winter shall
9 it be. And the LORD shall be king over all the earth: in that
10 day shall there be one LORD, and his name one. All the land shall be turned as a plain from Geba to Rimmon south of Jerusalem: and it shall be lifted up, and inhabited in her place, from Benjamin's gate unto the place of the first gate, unto the corner gate, and *from* the tower of Hananeel unto

8. With this verse begins the description of the actual blessings which this day will bring to God's people. The first figure used is that of *living waters*, that is, **waters running perennially from a fountain**, not standing pools, nor rain-filled streams, for these (Job vi. 16–18) do not flow *summer and winter* alike. The figure is significant, especially to the Oriental, of that kind of refreshment without which life must become extinct. It is the usual symbol with the prophets of the perennial flow of the life which proceeds from the living God; so here the waters *go out from Jerusalem, i.e.* from God's dwelling-place (cp. Joel iii. 18; Ezek. xlvii.; and Rev. xxii. 1). *The former sea* is the **Dead Sea**; *the hinder sea* is the **Mediterranean**. The whole land, east and west, shall be watered.

9. *The Lord shall be king over all the earth;* but the words rendered *all the earth* are those which in the next verse are rightly rendered *all the land*. It is very tempting, however, to accept this as a declaration that Jehovah will be universal King, known by one name among all nations. This is to be the great *result* of the world's history, of the world's experiences, and of the world's thought. It is not, as we might have expected, the starting-point. But that which all is to lead on and up to is, that men shall at last know and own their God and their unity in Him.

10. The purport of this verse is that the whole land shall be levelled or depressed so that Jerusalem may be left standing conspicuous. "The mountain of the Lord's house shall be established in the top of the mountains, and shall be exalted above the hills" (Isa. ii. 2). The natural site of Jerusalem gives it the appearance of being sunk in a hollow; for though itself built on an eminence, higher hills encompass it (Ps. cxxv. 2). But those surrounding hilly districts shall be made like a plain, lit. **like the Arabah**, of which Mr. Grove (Smith's *Dict.* i. 87) says: "This district has within our own times been identified with the deep-sunken valley or trench which forms the most striking among the many striking natural features of Palestine, and which extends with great uniformity of formation from the slopes of Hermon to the Elanitic gulf of the Red Sea; the most remarkable depression known to exist on the surface of the globe." *From Geba to Rimmon, i.e.* from the northern to the southern boundary of Judah, as the similar expression "from Geba to Beersheba" is used in 2 Kings xxiii. 8. Geba is the modern *Jeba*. Rimmon lay on the border of Edom, and is specified as *south of Jerusalem* to distinguish it from Rimmon in the north, in Galilee, and from the Rock of Rimmon in Benjamin. The land being thus levelled so as to leave the capital conspicuous, the city itself shall recover its old prosperity, and fill out its old dimensions. It *shall be inhabited in her place* . . . *the king's winepresses*. The landmarks here enumerated are not perfectly ascertained. The meaning

11 the king's winepresses. And *men* shall dwell in it, and there
shall be no more utter destruction; but Jerusalem shall be
12 safely inhabited. And this shall be the plague wherewith the
LORD will smite all the people that have fought against
Jerusalem; Their flesh shall consume away while they stand
upon their feet, and their eyes shall consume away in their
holes, and their tongue shall consume away in their mouth.
13 And it shall come to pass in that day, *that* a great tumult
from the LORD shall be among them; and they shall lay hold
every one on the hand of his neighbour, and his hand shall
14 rise up against the hand of his neighbour. And Judah also

is as if it had been said of Edinburgh, It shall be inhabited from the Braid
Hills to Trinity, and from Holyrood to Coltbridge. *Benjamin's gate* being
the exit towards the tribal district of that name, would naturally be on the
north-west of the city (where Barclay, *City of the Great King*, p. 153, puts it).
The *first gate* some would prefer translating **the oldest gate**, but this seems
unlikely, as another gate, situated not far from Benjamin's gate, was named
the old gate; and the likelihood is that this *first gate* (of which only *the place*
is mentioned) had been supplanted by *the corner gate*, a gate probably situated
near Hippicus on the western wall of the city, and 4000 cubits from the
Ephraim gate (2 Kings xiv. 13). *The tower of Hananeel* and *the king's winepresses* one would suppose were the landmarks on the extreme north and the
extreme south, but their site cannot be said to be ascertained (cp. Neh.
iii. 1, etc.).

11. *There shall be no more utter destruction*, there shall be no more curse,
Rev. xxii. 3. [The root signifies *to cut off*, hence *to devote*. It is the root that
appears in the word *Haram*, the name given to the devoted ground or sacred
enclosure round the Kaaba at Mecca, and round any mosque.]

12–19. These verses declare with what punishments those shall be visited
who have attacked the city of God or now refuse allegiance to her king. This
description of the plague-stricken people is shocking, but it is not more
shocking than what actually occurs (see Defoe's *Plague of London*). Kingsley
(*Life*, ii. 97) says: "What so terrible as war? I will tell you what is ten
times, and ten thousand times, more terrible than war, and that is—outraged
nature. Nature, insidious, inexpensive, silent, sends no roar of cannon, no
glitter of arms to do her work; she gives no warning note of preparation. . . .
Man has his courtesies of war, and his chivalries of war; he does not strike
the unarmed man; he spares the woman and the child. But nature . . .
spares neither woman nor child. . . . Silently she strikes the sleeping child,
with as little remorse as she would strike the strong man with the musket or
the pickaxe in his hand."

13. Examples of the disastrous results of panic would readily arise in the
Jewish mind (2 Chron. xx. 23; Judg. vii. 22). In the confusing movements
and smoke-thickened air of battle our own troops have sometimes fired on
allies, not recognising their uniforms; but this took place much more readily
in the vast armies of the East, of which the several contingents were differently
armed and ignorant of one another's languages.

14. "When Jehoshaphat and his people came to take away the spoil of

shall fight at Jerusalem; and the wealth of all the heathen round about shall be gathered together, gold, and silver, and
15 apparel, in great abundance. And so shall be the plague of the horse, of the mule, of the camel, and of the ass, and of all the beasts that shall be in these tents, as this plague.
16 And it shall come to pass, *that* every one that is left of all the nations which came against Jerusalem shall even go up from year to year to worship the King, the LORD of hosts,
17 and to keep the feast of tabernacles. And it shall be, *that*

them, they found among them in abundance both riches with the dead bodies and precious jewels which they stripped off for themselves, more than they could carry away; and they were three days in gathering the spoil, it was so much " (2 Chron. xx. 25).

15. The words of this verse inevitably recall Byron's on the destruction of Sennacherib's host in their encampment :

> " And there lay the steed with his nostril all wide,
> But through it there roll'd not the breath of his pride:
> And the foam of his gasping lay white on the turf,
> And cold as the spray of the rock-beating surf."

Had Byron seen a battle-field *before* he wrote these lines?

16. Keil thinks the *feast of Tabernacles* is mentioned because it was a feast of thanksgiving for the gracious protection of Israel in its wanderings through the desert and its introduction into the land flowing with milk and honey, whereby it foreshadowed the blessedness to be enjoyed in the kingdom of God (see also Michaelis). But in rejecting Koehler's observation that there is a reference to the feast as a harvest thanksgiving, he overlooks the fact, that if this harvest reference is not recognised, the punishment threatened in the next verse, the absence of rain, loses its appropriateness. The feast of Tabernacles was meant to keep them in mind amidst their abundant harvests and well-cared-for fields and vineyards, that as in the desert so still it was God who gave the increase. It was therefore a festival most suitable for all the nations to join in, by way of acknowledging that Jehovah was the God of nature throughout the earth, however various might be the aspects of nature with which they were familiar. Besides, there can be little doubt that by the time of Zechariah, and probably long before, this feast had become a kind of symbol of the ingathering of the nations (John iv. 35).

17. The withholding of rain was not only one of the ways by which idolatry and apostasy were punished under the theocracy (Wright; cp. 1 Kings xvii.), but it was the appropriate punishment of those who refused to acknowledge Jehovah as the giver of harvest. This suiting of punishment to offence is a marked characteristic of God's government, and should probably be more used in education than it is [*e.g.* by secluding for a time from all intercourse with his companions the boy who has told a lie, and so on]. Dante has largely utilized the principle in his great poem. In his vision of the realms of punishment he saw tyrants immersed in blood; gluttons exposed in all their pampered softness to a sleety tempest of cold, discoloured, stinking hail; the proud bending for ever under heavy burdens; schismatics who have rent the Church, themselves cleft asunder; those who had pried into the future and professed prophetic foresight, with faces reversed unable to see their own path.

whoso will not come up of *all* the families of the earth unto Jerusalem to worship the King, the LORD of hosts, even 18 upon them shall be no rain. And if the family of Egypt go not up, and come not, that *have* no *rain;* there shall be the plague, wherewith the LORD will smite the heathen that come 19 not up to keep the feast of tabernacles. This shall be the punishment of Egypt, and the punishment of all nations that 20 come not up to keep the feast of tabernacles. In that day shall there be upon the bells of the horses, HOLINESS UNTO THE LORD; and the pots in the LORD's house 21 shall be like the bowls before the altar. Yea, every pot in Jerusalem and in Judah shall be holiness unto the LORD of hosts: and all they that sacrifice shall come and take of them, and seethe therein: and in that day there shall be no more the Canaanite in the house of the LORD of hosts.

18. *And if the family . . . the plague.* The withholding of rain might be a punishment to other lands, but Egypt, depending on the Nile, might feel no alarm at this threat. Herodotus (ii. 13) tells us how the Egyptians pitied the Greeks when they heard they were dependent on rain, and supposed this very case: "If God shall some day see fit not to grant the Greeks rain, they will be swept away by famine, since they have no other resource for water." Sir J. G. Wilkinson remarks, however, that the roofs of the oldest temples at Thebes are fitted with lion's mouths to let the water run off. Lady Duff Gordon (*Letters*, p. 193) mentions that she had "a whole wet day—not known for ten years." This was in Upper Egypt. In Lower Egypt more rain falls. But the difficulty of the verse lies in the clause translated *that have no rain*, which is certainly incorrect. All things considered, the reading and translation of the LXX. seem to be best: **If the family of Egypt go not up and come not, even upon them shall be the plague with which the Lord will smite,** etc. If they scoff at the one punishment, the other will be sufficiently appalling. Even now the *plague* is the most alarming word to the Egyptians, who as lately as 1835, when Cairo lost one-third of its population, felt this terrible scourge (Lane, *Mod. Egyp.* i. 3, note).

20, 21. *Bells of the horses.* As with ourselves, so among ancient nations, grooms and drivers, either for ornament or use or both, decorated their horses with tassels and bells (Layard's *Nineveh*, ii. 28 and 358). The horses in Alexander's funeral procession had little gold bells attached to their cheek-straps. Now they were to be inscribed, not with figures of heathen gods or representations of commerce or the chase, but with the inscription *Holiness to the Lord*, which had hitherto been confined to the high priest's frontlet (Ex. xxviii. 36). Sacredness had been considered as attaching to that which was ceremonially set apart from all common use. But in the final state of God's people, the distinction between sacred and profane shall be abolished. All things shall be holy, nothing common nor unclean. The very *pots* in which the priests cooked their food would be as sacred as the *bowls* that caught the victim's blood. *Yea, every pot* (not only those in the temple) *in Jerusalem and in Judah shall be holiness to the Lord.* Observe (1) that the distinction between sacred and secular is to be abolished, but (2) not by separation from the world, not by ceasing to have anything to do with such demoralizing creatures as horses, nor by making all things secular, but by making all things holy, by carrying into all occupations the spirit of delight in God's presence. "Holiness to the Lord" is not to be obliterated from the high priest's mitre, so that he might feel as little solemnized when putting on his mitre and entering the holiest of all as if he were going into his stable to put the collar on his horse; but when he puts the collar on his horse and goes to his day's work or his day's recreation, he is to be as truly and lovingly at one with God as when with incense and priestly garments he enters the holy of holies. Finally, *there shall* in these days *be no more the Canaanite in the house of the Lord of hosts.* The term *Canaanite* is borrowed from the early days, when it conveyed the idea of all that was alien, hostile, unclean, and cursed. There shall enter in nothing that defileth.

> *How is the abolition of the distinction between sacred and secular brought about in fact? Illustrate this abolition from the life of Jesus, following Him in His various occupations, paying His taxes, eating and drinking, etc.*
>
> *Gather up from the prophets other spiritual features of the ultimate condition promised to God's people. Also collect the more external features by which the prophets characterized the day of the Lord.*
>
> *Compare the supreme and ultimate state which the prophets had in view with that depicted in the Book of Revelation, specifying particulars of comparison.*
>
> *Note some effects of the proclamation of God's unity, and its connection especially with the brotherhood of men.*
>
> *Illustrate the use of the word Canaanite in this passage by the use of* Philistine, miscreant, Frank, Kaffir.

INTRODUCTION

TO

THE BOOK OF MALACHI.

Of the personal history of the writer of this book nothing is known; so little, indeed, that within two centuries after these closing words of O. T. prophecy were uttered, the gravest doubts were entertained as to whether any individual had ever been known among men by the name of Malachi. For not only does the name never occur elsewhere in the O. T.; but, singularly enough, the word "Malachi" occurs in chap. iii. 1 (cp. ii. 7), and is there translated "my messenger," that is to say, it is there considered, and necessarily considered, an official title and not a personal name. Neither was this title an unknown one nor of novel application to the prophets of Jehovah. Haggai (i. 13) speaks of himself as "the messenger [*Malach*] of Jehovah." Accordingly, the Greek translators of the O. T. favour the opinion that "Malachi" is not a proper name; while some leading Jewish Rabbis, and some modern scholars of note, such as Vitringa and Hengstenberg, believed that Ezra was the author of this book, and was indicated thus in his capacity of prophet. Even so sagacious a critic as Calvin does not disapprove of this opinion, and it gains some further plausibility from the circumstance that Josephus, though giving a full account of the period, does not name Malachi.

It might perhaps be rash to form a quite decided opinion on such a point, yet as it was unquestionably usual for the prophets to give their own names in the title of their prophecies, the probability is that "Malachi" was the ordinary name of the prophet. [It would thus be the contracted form of Malachiah, Jehovah's messenger, following the analogy of Abi for Abijah, Uri for Urijah.] Deutsch observes: "A comparison of style and diction in Ezra and Malachi should, we think, prove sufficient to convince any scholar that they are written by very different hands." Ewald, while discountenancing the idea that Ezra was the author of this book (*Die Proph.* iii. 216), inclines to the opinion that Malachi is an assumed name, and that the superscription of the book (i. 1) is not by the hand of the author. Probably the safest opinion is that which Derenbourg expresses when he says: "The Chaldean version and the Talmud, which identify Malachi with Ezra, are guided by an unerring feeling of the truth; for if our prophet is not the great scribe himself, he is in any case the interpreter of his thought."[1]

In order to ascertain the date of this prophecy, we must find a period in Jewish history which was characterized by the existence of those abuses against which the words of the prophet were levelled. These abuses were a niggardly slovenliness amounting to profanity in the temple service,—the people withholding tithes and suitable offerings, the priests and Levites passing animals for sacrifice they should have rejected,—an unfaithfulness on the part of the priests to the responsibilities of their office, especially in the administration of the law; intermarriage with aliens; and a scepticism which was becoming bold and defiant. This is a state of society very different from that with which Zechariah had to do. The first zeal in connection with the restored temple has had time to cool. The lessons which Haggai taught regarding the connection between liberality and prosperity have died out with the generation that received them. We cannot look for such a state of matters much before the year 470 B.C., or, say, fifty years after the dedication of the restored temple.

But we have positive evidence that about this time these abuses had made their appearance. It was in the year 458-457 that Ezra visited Jerusalem, and that which dismayed and shocked him, prepared though he was to see many irregularities, was the scandalous extent to which both priests and people had intermarried with the heathen races around. He lay prostrate for hours, felled by the tidings as one who has received a heavy unexpected blow. But assured of his duty and of God's aid, and encouraged by the godly men who stood by him, he carried through a sweeping and thorough reform in this matter, and in a few months "made an end with all the men that had taken strange wives" (Ezra x. 17). But beyond this one reform there is no evidence that Ezra went or had occasion to go. There is no evidence that the scandals in the temple service of which Malachi speaks existed in Ezra's time, although, considering

[1] Derenbourg, *Histoire de la Palestine*, p. 22.

how many priests had intermarried with aliens, it is not improbable that in other respects also they were not immaculate. That the people were at this time in the poor and oppressed and half-starved condition which Malachi represents (iii. 5 and 11), is apparent from the fact that no sooner did Nehemiah arrive in Jerusalem a few years later, than the people came to him with the complaint (v. 3), "We have mortgaged our lands, vineyards, and houses, that we might buy corn, because of the dearth." Others had been obliged to sell their children as slaves in order to pay the enormous usury exacted by those to whom they were in debt (cp. Mal. ii. 10). But though it is possible that Malachi may have prophesied before Ezra came to Jerusalem (cp. Mal. iii. 16 with Ezra ix. 4; also Mal. iii. 6 and Ezra ix. 14, 15), yet the allusion (i. 4) to the vain attempt of Edom to rebuild their waste places must be held almost necessarily to imply that Israel had by this time succeeded in rebuilding their waste places, that is to say, that Jerusalem had already been restored by Nehemiah (cp. also ii. 13, note).

If Malachi did not prophesy before Ezra's visit, then no occasion for the use of such language as his arose again until the interval between the first and second visits of Nehemiah. In the twentieth year of Artaxerxes Longimanus [1] (445 B.C.), Nehemiah obtained leave of absence from the Persian court (where he filled the high post of cupbearer to the emperor), that he might visit Jerusalem, and if possible improve the miserable condition of his countrymen there. For the twelve succeeding years he acted as governor in Judea (Neh. v. 14), and during this time he thoroughly fortified Jerusalem, induced a larger proportion of the Jews to reside in it (Neh. vii. 4, xi. 1), and enforced several much-needed reforms in civil as well as in ecclesiastical matters. Especially he caused the whole population to enter into a solemn covenant, by which they engaged to observe the whole law of Moses, not to intermarry with aliens, to desist from trading on the seventh day, and to release creditors every seventh year, and, above all, to uphold by tithes and taxes the public service of God in the temple. After thus establishing and endowing religion, Nehemiah returned to the court of Persia in the year 433 B.C. How long his absence continued, he does not tell us (Neh. xiii. 6). It cannot have been long, for Artaxerxes, who died in 424 B.C., was still

---

[1] This does not mean, as Stanley seems to suppose, "of the Long arms," as if, like our Rob Roy, he could tie his garters without stooping; but "of the Long hand," because, as Plutarch says (*Artax.* i.) "he had the right hand longer than the left."

alive when he revisited Jerusalem; and yet it was long enough to reveal how slight a hold his reforms had taken on the character of the people. For on his return he found matters worse than ever, intermarriage with aliens countenanced by the family of the high priest, the temple service neglected and the tithes withheld, and Sabbath trading openly and regularly carried on. At this juncture again, therefore, the remonstrances of Malachi would find a fitting place, and it is to this date that a tolerably unanimous consent assigns them.[1] If this be the true date of Malachi, he must have uttered the first note of warning. For the steps taken by Nehemiah were so prompt, not to say vehemently swift, that no time seems to have intervened after his return during which the words of Malachi could have been listened to. But if we suppose that the prophet appeared slightly before Nehemiah's return, then the practical measures of the governor would seem to be the natural fulfilment and execution of the threats of the prophet. Nehemiah came "suddenly to the temple" and cleansed it (Neh. xiii. 8); he was "a swift witness" (xiii. 25) against all wrong-doers (Mal. iii. 5); he appeared in the spirit of Elijah (Mal. iv. 5), enforcing the law of Moses.

Whatever be the precise date of this prophecy, there is no doubt that Malachi has been justly styled "the Seal of the Prophets" or "the Last of the Prophets." The last three verses of the brief book form a strikingly suitable close to the O. T., pointing back, as they do, to the Law of Moses, which still underlay the whole experience of Israel, and which the prophets could only illustrate and enforce, and pointing forwards to the day when law and prophets should alike be merged in the personal manifestation of the Lord, and the word spoken and written be fulfilled in the Word Incarnate. "The last of the prophets, as he ends his work, does it with the sense that the mission of his order is for a time over, that there must be a revival of it in some age more or less distant, accompanied by great and terrible changes that should sweep away much that had been held as venerable and holy, but leading to a time of refreshment from the presence of the Lord, to a purer worship and a wider sense of brotherhood." This sense that the work of the prophets is coming to a close is apparent even in Zechariah. There is apparent in him a disposition to refer the people to the utterances of "the former

---

[1] Plumptre's article on "The Last of the Prophets" (*Biblical Studies*, p. 307) is, like everything else from his pen, very well worth reading, but it brings forward nothing which invalidates the evidence on which the opinion stated above is usually held.

prophets," and the experience of their fathers. These utterances and that experience had been such that admonition could no further go. The evils attendant on departure from God were written in such legible characters on their history that it could now have been justly said: "If they hear not Moses and the prophets, neither will they be persuaded though one rose from the dead."

Besides, the captivity had also taught the Jews the value of education and the power of an educated profession in a country. And when Ezra and his trained scribes came to Jerusalem and commenced their work of editing, publishing, explaining, and enforcing the law of Moses, it became obvious that there would now be less need for the living voice of prophets. Too much stress cannot be laid on the work of Ezra in connection with the law. Even Artaxerxes remarked upon it as if he always appeared with the law of God *in his hand*. And this becomes as it were the motto of the great change he introduced into the religious habits of his countrymen. Before his time, the prophet, the living voice, had been everything; after his time, the written law was all in all. Before his time, there appears to have been no arrangement for thoroughly instructing the people in the law; from his time, the law was carefully edited, copies of it were multiplied, trained teachers of it were scattered through the land, the people were summoned week by week to hear it, and thus the need of living prophets was the less felt. Looking at it from the human side, this marked change was similar to that through which a nation passes when its age of creative genius gives way to an age of learning, of criticism, and of history. The influential man in Israel was no longer the untutored peasant, sunburnt from the vineyard or the sheepfold, with the hairy garment and streaming locks of the prophet, denouncing the vices of the city on its public streets, and carrying men away for the moment with what their conscience told them was God's message to them; the influential man was now the well-washed, carefully-clad scribe, whose every movement and utterance were measured and decorous, and whose eye betokened not the enthusiasm of inspiration, but the calm judgment which education gives, and the self-confidence imparted by the possession of a number of technical details, the man who gave birth to the Pharisees with all their virtues and all their defects (cp. Ewald, Stanley, Monro).

Contents.—The book contains one prophecy which may be divided into three sections, with a few prefatory words. The Introduction

(i. 1–5) reminds Israel of the love God had shown them ; that the unreasonableness and ingratitude of their conduct may shame them :—

1. The priests are rebuked for despising God's name, polluting God's altar, behaving as uninterested hirelings. God therefore rejects their offerings, and declares that among the Gentiles His name will be honoured and worthy offerings rendered (i. 6–14). They are further rebuked for partiality in administering the law (ii. 1–9).

2. The people and priests are rebuked for intermarrying with idolatresses (ii. 9–16).

3. The people are rebuked for a scepticism that questioned moral distinctions and scoffed at the threatenings of judgment. The prophet reaffirms these threatenings, and promises ultimate blessing to those who adhere to obedience and hope (ii. 17–iv. 6).

MALACHI.

CHAPTER I.

1 THE burden of the word of the LORD to Israel by
2 Malachi. I have loved you, saith the LORD. Yet
ye say, Wherein hast thou loved us? *Was* not Esau Jacob's

TITLE AND INTRODUCTION (i. 1–5).

Jehovah affirms and proves His love for the people, that they may the rather be ashamed of their disregard and profane contempt of Him.

1. *The burden,* lit. **a burden.** The Hebrew word (*Massa*) is formed from a verb which means *to lift up, to bear,* and naturally therefore signifies that which is laid upon one to be borne. As we speak of laying a **charge** (*i.e.* etymologically, a *load*) against a prisoner, so this Hebrew word might mean an **accusation.** It might also mean a sentence or penalty or doom. And it has been observed that it is only used when the words uttered are condemnatory and threatening. (But cp. Prov. xxx. 1, xxxi. 1.) Others think it means simply **an utterance,** as we speak of a person *lifting up* his voice, or *taking up* his parable (cp. the Latin *ferunt*). A third meaning is suggested by our use of the word *burden,* when we speak of the burden of a song, or of what a person says; meaning its main drift or substance. It is in this sense the LXX. seem to have understood the word. (The *locus classicus* for ascertaining the meaning of the word is Jer. xxiii. 33–40.)

The message is to **Israel.** The nation has again resumed the name common to all the tribes. *By Malachi,* lit. **by the hand of Malachi** (cp. *Introduction to Malachi,* and Josh. xx. 2).

2. *I have loved you.* There is unfathomable pathos in the words which from time to time God has to use to justify Himself to His creatures. Cp. "I know the thoughts that I think towards you, thoughts of good and not of evil." He takes refuge, as it were, from the suspicions and doubts of His creatures in His own consciousness of His love for them. There is already implied in the emphatic *I have loved* you, the melancholy correlative, **but me ye have not loved.** *Yet ye say, Wherein hast thou loved us?* The insensibility of the people to their own spiritual condition is regularly exhibited in this book by the form of dialogue, the people being represented as asking in astonishment how they have shown the sin with which they are charged. "They have fallen into the last stage of selfish formalism when conscience ceases to do its work as an accusing witness, into the hypocrisy which does not even know itself to

3 brother? saith the LORD: yet I loved Jacob. And I hated Esau, and laid his mountains and his heritage waste for the
4 dragons of the wilderness. Whereas Edom saith, We are impoverished, but we will return and build the desolate places; thus saith the LORD of hosts, They shall build, but I will throw down; and they shall call them, The border of wickedness, and, The people against whom the LORD hath
5 indignation for ever. And your eyes shall see, and ye shall say, The LORD will be magnified from the border of Israel.

be hypocritical, the hypocrisy, in other words, of the Scribes and Pharisees" (Plumptre). If expanded, the querulous question of the people would run thus: Is it evidence of love, that after being 70 years subject as slaves to a cruel people, we should be suffered to return to freedom only that we might more keenly feel our own feebleness? Is it evidence of God's love that we have been left for well-nigh a century exposed to the scorn, violence, and robbery of troops of Ammonites and Samaritans? When our harvests are swept away by armed bands of marauders, when our seed is washed out of the ground by unseasonable rains, or rendered useless by mildew or drought, when we have to hear our children crying for bread we cannot give, and see their lips blue with famine, are we to find in these things evidences of God's love? God's reply is to point them to the much more calamitous condition of the nation nearest them in blood.

2-5. *Was not Esau . . . from the border of Israel.* The argument of these verses is this: If you would see the difference between hatred and love, look at the different condition and prospects of Edom and Israel. The desolation with which their territory is visited is irremediable: they have no glorious future beyond; whereas the wretched condition of which you complain is but the bleakness of seed-time that precedes the richest harvest. "Ye shall be a delightsome land: all nations shall call you blessed;" *The Lord will be magnified from the border of Israel* (cp. Ps. cxxix. 8), people will look to it as exhibiting clearer evidences of God's loving care than can elsewhere be discerned, but to Edom they shall point as *the border of wickedness*, **the country in whose history the career and end of the wicked** may be seen. And why this difference? You are brother-nations, starting from one womb. Is there anything to which you can refer the distinction but the fact that the one was loved, the other hated? *Dragons*, possibly **jackals**, possibly **scorpions**, which in large numbers actually infest the ruins in Edom. *Edom*, meaning **Red** (cp. Gen. xxv. 30). [With this prediction of permanent desolation in Edom, compare Obadiah; Isa. xxxiv.; Jer. xlix.; Ezek. xxv. 13. Its fulfilment is traced in the *History of Edom* by Keith, pp. 192-245. For the wider application which Paul makes of the fact that God loved the one brother and hated the other, see Rom. ix. 13, and the commentaries on that chapter, but especially Pfleiderer's *Paulinism*, i. 245, Eng. Tr.]

REMARKS.—The frequent introduction of dialogue in Malachi indicates at once moral insensibility and intellectual activity on the part of the people. A questioning spirit had grown up among them which threatened to subvert and confound even fundamental moral distinctions. Compare the fine passage

6 A son honoureth *his* father, and a servant his master: if then I *be* a father, where *is* mine honour? and if I *be* a master, where *is* my fear? saith the LORD of hosts unto you, O priests, that despise my name. And ye say, Wherein have

in Burke (Payne's edition, ii. 101), beginning, "We know that *we* have made no discoveries, and we think that no discoveries are to be made, in morality; nor many in the great principles of government, nor in the ideas of liberty, which were understood long before we were born, altogether as well as they will be after the grave has heaped its mould on our presumption, and the silent tomb shall have imposed its law on our pert loquacity." The whole of this most masculine passage carries a weighty warning to our own generation.

> *Why is it no use trying to discover where "the lost tribes" are?*
> *What signs of an advanced stage of national corruption do you discern in this book?*
> *Specify other prophecies against Edom, and mark their distinguishing features. What Psalm alludes to the unfriendly conduct of Edom?*
> *On what occasion was the threat of* ver. *4 very strikingly fulfilled in the case of* Israel *after their rejection of the Messiah?*
> *Give the different names, poetical as well as ordinary, of Edom. Give other scriptural instances of similarly-derived names.* [*Peniel, Gilgal, etc.*]
> *What is the meaning of* Esau? [Cp. *Ursula.*]
> *Name any great cities of Edom, and say what they are remarkable for.*
> *What Edomite played a distinguished part in Israel's history?*
> *Show the difference between the argument of this passage and that which Tennyson refutes in the stanza:*
>
> > 'That loss is common would not make
> > My own less bitter, rather more:
> > Too common! Never morning wore
> > To evening, but some heart did break.'

THE PRIESTS REBUKED (i. 6–ii. 9).

This section is so closely connected in all its parts, and is so pervaded throughout by the same ideas, that it is not easy to break it up without letting some of its significance escape. It may perhaps best be divided into three paragraphs: (1) The priests are charged with showing their contempt for God's name by offering worthless, cheap sacrifices (i. 6–8). (2) God declares He will reject their services, and find among the heathen those who will reverence His name (i. 9–14). (3) The priests shall be punished for their contempt by themselves being made contemptible (ii. 1–9).

6. *A son honoureth his father*, lit. **son will honour father**; which some suppose to mean **ought to honour**, but probably the E. V. is correct. [Aristotle says the son must always be his father's debtor, because he can never repay him for those greatest of all benefits, birth and upbringing; and in this, he says, fathers resemble God (*Eth. Nic.* viii. 12, 14).] *If then I be a father.* Cp. Ex. iv. 22, "Israel is my son, my first-born." See also Deut. xxxii. 6; Isa. lxiii. 16. *Where is my fear*, where **is the reverential awe that is due to me?** *saith the Lord of hosts*, etc., **saith Jehovah of hosts unto you priests, despisers of my name, yet ye say.**

I. 9.]   THE PRIESTS REBUKED.   137

7 we despised thy name? Ye offer polluted bread upon mine altar; and ye say, Wherein have we polluted thee? In that
8 ye say, The table of the LORD *is* contemptible. And if ye offer the blind for sacrifice, *is it* not evil? and if ye offer the lame and sick, *is it* not evil? offer it now unto thy governor; will he be pleased with thee, or accept thy person? saith the
9 LORD of hosts. And now, I pray you, beseech God that he will be gracious unto us: this hath been by your means: will

7, 8. *Ye offer polluted bread.* This is not an answer to the question with which ver. 6 concludes, but is a second predicate descriptive of the priests, and added to that given in the words *despisers of my name.* This is shown in the Hebrew construction, and might be represented thus:

> Saith Jehovah unto you priests,
> Despisers of my name;
> Yet ye say, Wherein have we despised thy name?
> Offerers of polluted bread on mine altar;
> Yet ye say, Wherein have we polluted thee?

(Then follows the answer.) "By your saying, The table of the Lord is contemptible, and (by your saying) when you offer the blind for sacrifice, It is no evil [**nothing wrong**]," etc. The *yet ye say* introduces in each case the added accusation of moral insensibility; and their saying, **The table of the Lord is despicable**, is the reply to the first question, and **when ye offer the blind** to the second. *Bread*, **food, meat,** here includes all offerings by fire on the altar (cp. Lev. xxi. 6; Ezek. xliv. 7); the altar being here signified by the word *table*, as in Ezek. xli. 22 and xliv. 16. The sin with which the priests are charged is that of polluting God's altar by offering beasts not ceremonially clean, unfit for sacrifice. Any beast was passed as good enough for sacrifice, the lame or blind that had become useless for work, the sick or torn, the beast that was dying on its feet, and could not be used for meat, or that which had been stolen, and so marked that it would not sell—anything, in short, that could serve no other purpose was good enough for God. His courts had the appearance of a knacker's yard. *Offer it now unto thy governor.* When you wish a boon from the Persian Pasha, will you try to ingratiate yourself and secure his favour by making him a gift of such wretched skeletons as he sees driven limping into the temple? The custom alluded to, that of taking a gift in the hand or sending it on before when one comes to ask a favour, is perhaps too well understood to need illustration; but Burton's words (*Pilgrimage*, i. 29) may be cited: "There are three ways of treating Asiatic officials, by bribe, by bullying, or by bothering them with a dogged perseverance into attending to you and your concerns."

9. This sentence is ironical: Ye dare not go before your governor with such presents; but come now, I pray you, enter God's presence and use your stock phrase of supplication (cp. Num. vi. 25) "that He would be gracious unto us." Will He regard your persons? The clause rendered *this hath been by your means*, is literally **from your hand hath been this**, which certainly may mean, **this abuse has arisen through your fault**; but which, considering the lively abrupt style of the verse, much more probably means **from your hand comes this scurvy offering.** The verse calls upon the priests to come

10 he regard your persons? saith the LORD of hosts. Who *is there* even among you that would shut the doors *for nought*? neither do ye kindle *fire* on mine altar for nought. I have no pleasure in you, saith the LORD of hosts, neither will I
11 accept an offering at your hand. For from the rising of the sun even unto the going down of the same my name *shall be* great among the Gentiles; and in every place incense *shall be* offered unto my name, and a pure offering: for my name *shall be* great among the heathen, saith the LORD of hosts.
12 But ye have profaned it, in that ye say, The table of the LORD *is* polluted; and the fruit thereof, *even* his meat, *is*
13 contemptible. Ye said also, Behold, what a weariness *is it!* and ye have snuffed at it, saith the LORD of hosts; and ye brought *that which was* torn, and the lame, and the sick;

as usual to pray God in the people's behalf; but what offering do they bring to propitiate God? From your hand this! this wretched creature is what I am to accept!

10. *Who ... for nought*, rather, **Would that there were also some one among you that would shut the doors, that ye might not kindle fire on mine altar in vain.** As if God were to say, It were far better that the temple were shut than that such profane and fruitless worship were carried on in it (cp. Isa. i. 12: "Who hath required this at your hand, to tread my courts? Bring no more vain oblations," etc.). Better that you and your offensive beasts be together shut out of the temple, and that no smoke ascend from the altar, since all such offerings as you present are offered in vain. The Hebrew word translated *for nought* is the etymological equivalent of *gratis*; but the meaning here is not *without reward*, but the closely allied, secondary meaning, *without result*: it is not the mercenary but the fruitless character of the services which is pointed at.

11. This prediction differs from the usual O. T. prophecy regarding the ingathering of the Gentiles by its emphasizing the antecedent rejection of the Jews. For the fulfilment, see notes on Zech. viii. 20–23; and cp. especially Acts xiii. 46. The words *in every place* point to the time of which our Lord said, "The hour cometh when ye shall neither in this mountain, nor yet at Jerusalem, worship the Father," etc. (John iv. 20–24). *Incense*, the O. T. clothing is used even for the N. T. idea. The words *among the heathen* and *among the Gentiles* represent the same Hebrew word.

12. This verse is a repetition of the accusation conveyed in ver. 7, suggested by the words of ver. 11, *My name shall be great among the heathen:* **but as for you, ye profane it by your saying, Jehovah's table, it is polluted; and its fruit, despicable [worthless] is it for eating.** The beasts sacrificed were so poor that even the parts which fell to be eaten by the priests seemed to them not worth having, scarcely wholesome or good for food. The expression *the fruit thereof* is rendered by the LXX. *the things set [laid] upon the altar* (cp. Lev. vi. 16, vii. 32–34, etc.).

13. *Ye said also, Behold what a weariness!* The LXX. translate: "Behold, these are out of our affliction;" and are followed by the Vulgate, as if the people were represented as apologizing for the poor-looking beasts by

thus ye brought an offering : should I accept this of your
14 hand? saith the LORD. But cursed *be* the deceiver, which
hath in his flock a male, and voweth, and sacrificeth unto the
Lord a corrupt thing : for I *am* a great King, saith the LORD
of hosts, and my name *is* dreadful among the heathen.

pleading their afflicted condition, and that their poverty could furnish no better. Another translator renders this and the following clause as if those who brought the offerings expressed a feigned weariness, and puffed and panted as if burdened by the heavy, well-fed beast, and threw it down, saying, "Behold, what a weight it is!" while all the time the beast was so light it might be blown away. These interpretations are interesting, but our own version is correct : **What a burden the service of God is!** " The service of God is its own reward. If not, it becomes a greater toil, with less reward from this earth than the things of this earth. Our only choice is between love and weariness" (Pusey). The *torn* should rather be the **stolen**. That which was worried by beasts might not be offered in sacrifice, but it had a special name, not the word here used.

14. *Cursed be the deceiver.* Not the man who openly denies God, and makes no pretence of serving Him, but the man who seeks to stand well with God and yet to be at no expense in the matter. *Which hath in his flock a male.* For if he had nothing to offer, nothing would be expected of him—nay, even though he had a male in his flock, the law might not require it from him ; but the unreal worshipper is often apparently zealous and *voweth*, steps beyond the law and makes an ostentation of liberality, and yet, though he has *vowed* what is perfect, *sacrificeth unto the Lord a corrupt thing* (cp. the characteristic points in the conduct of Ananias and Sapphira). But "God is not mocked ;" these profane and insolent ways merely deceive those who practise them. They justly incur a *curse*. *For I am a great King, and my name is dreadful* [or, in correspondence with the previous occurrence of the cognate word in ver. 6, **to be feared**] *among the heathen*. The feeling of love to God is needful, but it must be combined with deep reverence if men are to be upheld in that attitude of spirit which befits them. Decay of reverential awe involves decay of much that is essential to godliness—involves even the decay of love itself. [Contrast with the conduct denounced in this verse that which Shammai enjoined in the words, "Say little and do much. Be like Abraham, who only promised *a morsel of bread*, but fetched *a calf tender and good*" (*Pirke Aboth*, I. 16).]

CHAPTER II.

1 AND now, O ye priests, this commandment *is* for you.

1. *This commandment.* Keil supposes that this refers to the threatening contained in vers. 2, 3. "The term *command*," he says, "is applied to that which the Lord has resolved to bring upon a person, inasmuch as the execution or accomplishment is effected by earthly instruments by virtue of a divine

2 If ye will not hear, and if ye will not lay *it* to heart, to give glory unto my name, saith the LORD of hosts, I will even send a curse upon you, and I will curse your blessings: yea, I have cursed them already, because ye do not lay *it* to
3 heart. Behold, I will corrupt your seed, and spread dung upon your faces, *even* the dung of your solemn feasts; and
4 *one* shall take you away with it. And ye shall know that I have sent this commandment unto you, that my covenant
5 might be with Levi, saith the LORD of hosts. My covenant

command." It might suitably be rendered, "This decree, this fiat or decision which I have uttered, and now gather up in one final denunciation" (cp. Lev. xxv. 21).

2. *I will curse your blessings*, **your benedictions.** Not the personal advantages and perquisites enjoyed by the priests, but the blessings they pronounced upon the people. Their service had been merely formal without any soul of reverence in it: the blessings they uttered should retributively be evacuated of all efficacy, and should be a mere formula.

3. *I will corrupt your seed.* Ewald, Keil, and others follow the LXX. in adopting a slightly different reading, which affords the meaning: **I will rebuke [wither] your arm**, as if the arm stretched out to bless the people should be withered. Comparison with similar passages in the prophets seems rather to indicate that our reading and version are correct; but the context here is strongly in favour of this suggested emendation; for the prophet has not only threatened that the blessings uttered by the priests should turn to curses, but he goes on to declare that instead of the people looking upon the priest with awe as he came out from the presence of God to bless them, and as it were to shine on them with his face, *dung* should be *spread upon the faces* of the priests, the dung of their sacrificial animals.

4. *And ye shall know . . . with Levi.* When the judgment of God falls upon the priests, they shall recognise His hand in the contempt in which they are held. But the next clause should be rendered, **to be my covenant with Levi**, meaning that this decree issued against the priests is now to take the place of the old covenant with Levi; this is what God now engages Himself to do to them and by them; and the priests themselves should recognise this: **Ye shall know that I have sent this commandment unto you, to be my covenant with Levi.**

5-7. These verses describe what the covenant with Levi *had been.* The construction of ver. 5 has given rise to three interpretations—(1) that of our version; (2) that of the Vulgate, Luther, Ewald (following the LXX., which is similar): *I gave to him fear that he might fear me;* (3) and best, the sense suggested by Moore: "My covenant with Levi was this, namely, on my part there were to be given to him life and peace; and I fulfilled my part, and gave them to him: on his part there was to be rendered to me reverence; and he did reverence me, and fear before my name." The translation, then, will be:

"My covenant was with him
Life and peace, and I gave them to him:
Fear, and he feared me,
And trembled before my name."

was with him of life and peace; and I gave them to him *for the fear wherewith he feared me, and was afraid before my* 6 *name.* The law of truth was in his mouth, and iniquity was not found in his lips: he walked with me in peace and equity, 7 and did turn many away from iniquity. For the priest's lips should keep knowledge, and they should seek the law at his 8 mouth: for he *is* the messenger of the LORD of hosts. But ye are departed out of the way; ye have caused many to stumble at the law; ye have corrupted the covenant of Levi, 9 saith the LORD of hosts. Therefore have I also made you contemptible and base before all the people, according as ye have not kept my ways, but have been partial in the law.

That is to say, on both sides the covenant was kept. The covenant was definitely made with Levi (*i.e.* with the tribe, not the individual) on the occasion recorded in Num. xxv. (cp. Deut. xxxiii. 9).

6. Further commendation of the primitive priesthood. The priests were appointed to teach Israel the law (Deut. xxxiii. 10), especially by acting as judges, and so applying and enforcing it (Deut. xvii. 9, xix. 17). This the priests in old times had faithfully done. *The law of truth was in his mouth.* They had also been themselves living embodiments of the wholesome instruction they gave to others. *He walked with me in peace and equity, and did turn many away from iniquity.* The same commendation is found in the *Pirke Aboth* (i. 13): "Hillel said: Be of the disciples of Aaron, loving peace, and pursuing peace; loving mankind and bringing them nigh to Thorah" (cp. *Pirke*, i. 19: "On three things the world stands; on Judgment, and on Truth, and on Peace"). On the last clause of the verse, Pusey remarks: "What a history of zeal for the glory of God and of the conversion of sinners in those of whom the world knows nothing, of whose working, but for the three words in the closing book of the O.T., we should have known nothing."

7. What these commended priests did, they did in conformity with the responsibilities of their office, and the terms of the fundamental covenant. *For the priest's lips should keep knowledge . . . for he is the messenger of the Lord of hosts.* The priest is here called, as elsewhere the prophet is called, the *messenger*, the *angel* of Jehovah, through whom and by whom Jehovah speaks to and acts upon men. Such were the priests with whom God had made and to whom He had kept His covenant.

8. *But ye are departed out of the way.* Ye are very different in your conduct from the ideal priest, and even from your actual predecessors in office. Your careless teaching, your superficial dealing, your contentment with formulas and external rites, and your personal laxity, have given men a prejudice against religion altogether. Instead of helping men to accept the truth and live godly, you have caused even those who wished to do so to take offence and turn away. A sceptical age is necessarily the result of externality and heartlessness in the religious teachers of previous generations.

9. The priests having broken covenant with God, He makes them *contemptible and base before all the people* (cp. Micah iii. 11). "It is righteous with God that ministers hunting after honour, applause, and estimation, by partiality and pleasing of men, do by that very mean come in contempt" (Hutcheson).

REMARKS.—1. "God assures these Jews that a cheap religion, like most cheap things, is always dear, since it always costs more than it is worth—for it is worth just nothing" (Moore).

2. There is no middle place between finding God's service a burden and finding in it the simple expression of a loving devotedness. Only when sacrifices are the willing, coveted expressions of a regard for God are they acceptable. Only what you *like* to give does God like to receive. Your gladness in the giving is the measure of His gladness in receiving. All worshippers who come with no alacrity but as if they were driven into His house, as the Jews used to be driven into Christian churches in the Dark Ages, are assured that their worship is no pleasure to God. He would rather see His courts empty than filled with such worshippers. Shut the doors, He says, and keep these people out.

3. Observe the insolence of profanity, and its folly, thinking to propitiate God by insult. The pre-Islamic Arabs when gathering the first-fruits, if any fell from the idol's portion into God's portion, restored it; but if any fell from God's to the idol's, they left it there. So when they watered the idol's grounds, if the water broke over the channels and watered God's portion, they dammed it up again; but if the channels on God's ground broke and let the water irrigate the idol's ground, they let it run on.

> *Collect passages from the O. T. illustrating the use of the expression*, The name of the Lord.
> *In what sense is God called a Father in the O. T., and what enlargement of that sense is introduced by the Incarnation?*
> *George Hutcheson in commenting on this passage says:* "*The very respect which is paid as due to creatures, will be a ditty against sleighters of God.*" *What does he mean by* ditty, *and what word from the same root would we use?*
> *What qualifications did the Mosaic law require in sacrificial animals, and what was the significance of these qualifications?*
> Gentiles. *Give the names used by other races to indicate foreigners* [e.g. *Barbarians, Welsh, etc.*].
> *Commit to memory the hymn,* "*Jesus, where'er thy people meet.*"

INTERMARRIAGE WITH ALIENS DENOUNCED (ii. 10-16.)

This paragraph may be connected with the preceding by the idea of the *covenant* which is prominent in both. The priests have been charged with breach of the Levitical covenant: the people are now charged with that breach of their national covenant which was then specially scandalous and dangerous—intermarriage with idolatrous women. Both Ezra and Nehemiah viewed these alliances with the intensest horror and alarm. It is true that alien blood ran in the veins of David himself, but the Moabitish ancestress of the royal house was not an idolatress. No such antipathy to marriage with foreigners seems to have prevailed during the age of Solomon; but even in his age the calamitous results of such marriages were sufficiently obvious, and in the post-exilian times the very existence of God's people was imperilled by the growing prevalence of the custom. Malachi recognises it as the danger of his generation. He denounces it as unpatriotic, as thwarting God's purpose in making them a separate people, and as leading to cruelly facile divorce.

10 Have we not all one father? hath not one God created us? why do we deal treacherously every man against his brother,
11 by profaning the covenant of our fathers? Judah hath dealt treacherously, and an abomination is committed in Israel and in Jerusalem; for Judah hath profaned the holiness of the LORD which he loved, and hath married the daughter of
12 a strange god. The LORD will cut off the man that doeth this, the master and the scholar, out of the tabernacles of Jacob, and him that offereth an offering unto the LORD of
13 hosts. And this have ye done again, covering the altar of the LORD with tears, with weeping, and with crying out, insomuch that he regardeth not the offering any more, or

10. *Have we . . . created us?* Here, as in chap. i. 6, the prophet, before giving any hint of its application, first lays down the principle. We Israelites have all one father; we are the children of God in a peculiar sense. One God has created us; so indeed has one God created all men, but us He has created for special purposes and by peculiar operations (cp. Isa. xliii. 7, "I have created him for my glory;" also Ex. iv. 22). We are bound together not merely by the ordinary ties of fellow-citizenship, but by being partakers in a special relation to God and a special covenant with Him. *Why*, then, *do we deal treacherously every man against his brother*—that is, as vers. 11, 14, and 15 show, Why do we repudiate Jewish wives to make room for aliens? By doing so, *we profane the covenant of our fathers*—that is, we introduce among the holy nation sprinkled with the blood of the covenant, women who worship idols and practise abominable customs in the name of religion (cp. Neh. xiii. 23–29; Ezra ix. 2, 11–14; Num. xxv.).

11. The charge implied in the former verse is here explicitly made; and the *gravamen* of the charge is indicated in the designation of the alien woman, *the daughter of a strange god, i.e.* an idolatress. It was by marrying idolatresses that the people of *Judah profaned the holiness of the Lord which he loved,* or brought down to the common earthly level the holy people (Jer. ii. 3) whom Jehovah loved, and in whom His holiness was meant to be manifested.

12. Judgment is pronounced upon the sin. Utter extermination is threatened. But the expression is of doubtful meaning, *the master and the scholar.* Gesenius translates one wakeful and one answering, *i.e.* "every one who is alive—a proverbial phrase, perhaps taken from the Levites keeping watch in the temple, one of whom watches and calls out, and the other answers. In the same sense the Arabs say, *no one crying out and no one answering."* The reference to the temple watch seems needless; its origin was probably more general. Cp. the expressions "bond and free," "rich and poor," "root and branch." *And him that offereth.* This completes the total of Israel's population; he that appears in Zion as well as he who dwells in the tents of Jacob shall be cut off (cp. Ps. lxxxvii. 2). The facts recorded by Nehemiah are strongly in favour of the idea that the priests are especially meant (Neh. xiii. 28).

13. *And this have ye done again, i.e.* a second time. Even after the reformation accomplished by Ezra (Ezra x.), and the solemn covenant entered into

14 receiveth *it* with good will at your hand. Yet ye say, Wherefore? Because the LORD hath been witness between thee and the wife of thy youth, against whom thou hast dealt treacherously : yet *is* she thy companion, and the wife of thy 15 covenant. And did not he make one? Yet had he the residue of the spirit. And wherefore one? That he might seek a godly seed. Therefore take heed to your spirit, and let none deal treacherously against the wife of his youth.

under Nehemiah (Neh. ix. 10), ye have repeated the offence (Neh. xiii.). Malachi notes a feature of the case which Nehemiah omits, the misery occasioned to the Jewish wives, who were either divorced that foreign women might take their place, or were despised and ill-used by the interlopers. It was this deep, concealed anguish or loud, bitter wailing that arose to God, mingling with the Pharisaic service of the husband, and making it offensive to God. The women, abandoned by their natural protectors, flee to God's altar as their refuge, and pour out their grief and wrongs to Him.

14. *Yet ye say, Wherefore?* Why does God reject our offerings? Again the prophet uses their moral insensibility as an occasion for more explicitly pressing home their guilt. *Because the Lord hath been witness.* There seems to have been no religious service accompanying marriages under the O. T. ; but even without being formally invoked, God observed how the marriage contract was kept. Cp. the solemn adjuration of Laban : "The Lord watch between me and thee, when we are absent one from another. If thou shalt afflict my daughters, *or if thou shalt take other wives beside my daughters*, no man is with us; see, God is witness between me and thee" (Gen. xxxi. 49, 50).

15. *And did . . . a godly seed.* The Authorized Version of this obscure verse is sometimes accepted as signifying : Did not God make one, *i.e.* one Eve for Adam ? Yet had He the residue of the spirit, power to make many wives for him, had He so pleased. Why then did He make but one? That a godly seed might be secured, an object defeated where there is plurality of wives. To this interpretation, however, there are fatal objections in the Hebrew. Another rendering has therefore been widely accepted : **And has no one done this who has a remnant of spirit in him ?**—this being one of the questions with which the prophet supposes himself to be interrupted by the Jews, and to which he replies, knowing that they have the conduct of Abraham in view : **Wherefore did the one so act ?** He did so, **seeking a godly seed.** He took Hagar in addition to Sarah, under the impression that he could thus raise a seed to inherit God's promises, a very different object from that which Malachi's contemporaries could plead. **Take heed therefore to your spirit.** See that your conscience be as clear as Abraham's in this matter.

But the interpretation that has most in its favour is thus explained by Moore : "The prophet at the outset had argued the oneness of the Jewish people from the fact that they had one father. They were therefore one, and these mixed marriages that violated this oneness were wrong. This wrong becomes more apparent when the reason for this oneness is regarded. Having then shown that the Jews were breaking this arrangement, and inflicting cruel injustice on their covenant wives, he asks again, as he did at the outset, 'Did not God make us one ? Did He not separate us from other nations into an isolated unity ?' Yet this was not done because the blessing

16 For the LORD, the God of Israel, saith that he hateth putting away: for *one* covereth violence with his garment, saith the LORD of hosts: therefore take heed to your spirit, that ye deal not treacherously.

was too narrow to be spread over other nations, or because infinite fulness was exhausted; for the residue of the Spirit was with Him. There remained an inexhaustible fulness of spiritual blessing that might have been given to other nations. Why, then, did He choose but one? It was that He might make a seed of God, a nation which He should train to be the repository of His covenant and the stock of His Messiah, a people in which the true doctrine of the unity of God should be cherished amid surrounding polytheism and idolatry, until the fulness of time should come. Now to introduce this very polytheism and idolatry into the chosen people, and to reject the wives who were protected by the covenant, was to break up this oneness, and do that which, if persisted in, would amalgamate the Jewish people with the other nations of the earth."

16. *For the Lord . . . putting away*, better, **For I hate divorce, saith Jehovah, God of Israel.** The following clause is literally: **And he** [the man who divorces his wife to marry another] **covereth his garment with violence;** but as the Arabs use the word *garment* to denote *a wife* ("Wives are your attire, and you are theirs," Koran, *Sur.* ii.), and as the Hebrew customs point in the same direction (cp. Deut. xxii. 30; Ruth iii. 9), the expression is commonly accepted as meaning **he does violence to his wife.** This is specious, but it would be better to suppose a reference to the splendid wedding garment which to the discerning eye appeared now stained with unmanly violence, as if with blood stains. *Take heed that ye deal not treacherously.* Observe the recurrence of this expression as the refrain of the paragraph, vers. 10, 11, 14, 15, 16.

REMARKS.—1. Since first the law had been given, it never received, not even in Israel's best days, a more signal homage than when those who had married foreign wives repudiated them at the instigation of Ezra. The people that could thus sacrifice their keenest personal feelings to the national welfare had still in them a strength of character which must have gladdened the heart of any ruler, and proved them yet capable of a great future. And yet they fell back into the same sin again.

2. "They made an end with all the men that had taken strange wives." What agonized pleading of wife with husband, and of mother for her children; what passages of wild entreaty, reproach, and fondest love; what complications of miseries, anxieties about the future, unveilings of a hitherto disguised past; what strife between the purest affections and a sense of duty; what givings way and returns to a better mind; what violent openings up of every man's heart, are all covered over by this bare historical expression! Two companion pictures might be drawn, the one of the putting away of the Jewish wives, the other of the enforced banishment of the foreign wives.

3. Mohammed, too, is reported to have said: "God has not created anything on earth which He likes better than the emancipating of slaves, nor has He created anything which He dislikes more than divorce." Yet it is a principle of Mohammedan law that "a husband may divorce his wife without any misbehaviour on her part, or without assigning any cause." The husband has

17   Ye have wearied the LORD with your words. Yet ye say, Wherein have we wearied *him*? When ye say, Every one that doeth evil *is* good in the sight of the LORD, and he delighteth in them; or, Where *is* the God of judgment?

only to utter a certain form of words and pay the wife her dowry, and she is no longer his wife.

4. Observe the sacredness of family life, as the nursery of a "seed of God."

Explain why intermarriage with aliens was prohibited to the Jews, and mention some occasions on which great calamity followed such marriages.

In what sense were the Jews a peculiar people? Were they God's children in a different sense from that in which other nations were the children of God? What originally constituted them a distinct people and a nation separate from other nations?

What was the Jewish law regarding divorce, and what amendment of it was introduced by our Lord?

Cite from the N. T. an instance of a woman who had apparently been the victim of facile divorce.

Give some account of the Jewish marriage ceremony and feast.

THE COMING OF THE GOD OF JUDGMENT (ii. 17–iv. 6).

In Malachi's time there was a questioning spirit abroad. What the Jews had seen and learned in captivity by mingling with foreigners had suggested to them many new views of things, and had infected at least a part of the population with a sceptical tone. They turned upon their own faith a more daringly critical eye; they accustomed themselves to measure the promises of God and the utterances of the prophets by the facts of life; and when they found that the innocent were often involved with the guilty in a common disaster, they were forward to say, Where is the God of judgment? Where is the God that promised through Haggai and Zechariah to come speedily to His people? This tone of thought finds an elaborate expression in the book of Ecclesiastes, and it is directly and vigorously met in this paragraph of Malachi—first, by the renewed declaration that the Lord will come, but will come in an unexpected time and an unexpected manner, with judgment (iii. 1–5); secondly, by the explanation that the delay in the fulfilment of God's promises was due not to any change in Him, but to their disbelief and neglect, which made it impossible for Him to find access to them (iii. 6–12); thirdly, by the intimation that when He does come the difference between the God-fearing and the contumacious and sceptical will be sufficiently marked (iii. 13–iv. 3). The prophecy concludes, fourthly, with a brief exhortation to adhere to the law, and a renewed promise that in order to prepare a people for the coming Lord, a prophet shall be sent who shall be a second Elijah for boldness and vigour.

17. This is addressed to the people as a whole, although iii. 16 shows that there were individuals who had not spoken unadvisedly with their lips (cp. Isa. xliii. 24). Samples of the outspoken unbelief, or at least bitter perplexities which men were fond of uttering, and which **wearied** God, are given here

and in iii. 14, 15. The book of Job and the 73d Psalm give utterance to similar perplexities. They will always be felt where men go on the presumption that *immediate* punishment ought to be inflicted on evil-doers, and *present* prosperity be the reward of the righteous. The evil prosper, therefore God delights in them; *or*, **if this be not the case**, if He does not take pleasure in the wicked, why does He not appear as God of judgment? Part of the difficulty is thus put by the great exponent of modern perplexities:

" Yet, even when man forsakes
All sin—is just, is pure,
Abandons all which makes
His welfare insecure—
Other existences there are, that clash with ours.

" Streams will not curb their pride
The just man not to entomb,
Nor lightnings go aside
To give his virtues room;
Nor is that wind less rough which blows a good man's barge."

CHAPTER III.

1 BEHOLD, I will send my messenger, and he shall prepare the way before me: and the Lord, whom ye seek, shall suddenly come to his temple, even the messenger of the covenant, whom ye delight in: behold, he shall come, saith the LORD

1. *Behold, I will send my messenger*, or, **I send my messenger** [*Malachi*]. This and the following verses are the reply to the sceptical question, Where is the God of judgment? In the first place, a preparatory work was needed before God could come to His people. They were not in a fit state to receive Him. The delay of which they complained was occasioned not by indifference on His part, but on theirs (cp. vers. 6-12). The messenger who prepared the way for the personal advent of the Lord was John the Baptist (cp. Matt. iii. 3, and parallel passages). The definition of his work as *a preparing of the way* is derived from Isa. xl. 3. [For the figure, cp. Stanley's *Through the Dark Cont.* i. 198: "The road had been prepared for his Imperial Majesty's hunting excursion, and was 8 feet wide, through jungle and garden, forest and field."] When the way is prepared, then **the Lord** [usually, *the Lord* in the English Version represents the word *Jehovah* in the original, but here it is another word it represents—a word which means the owner or lord; *he* shall come to the temple whose right it is to cleanse it, because it is his], **whom ye seek** [whose absence you scoffingly remark upon, or murmuringly complain of, and whose presence and judgment you invite], **shall suddenly come to his temple**, like the priest whose duty it was to superintend the temple arrangements, and who might at any moment knock and demand admittance. "He came," says Edersheim (*Temple*, 120), "suddenly and unexpectedly, no one knew when. The Rabbis say, Sometimes he came at the cock-crowing, sometimes a little earlier, sometimes a little later. He came and knocked, and they opened to him. Then said he unto them, All ye who have washed, come and cast lots," *i.e.* for the privilege of ministering

2 of hosts. But who may abide the day of his coming? and who shall stand when he appeareth? for he *is* like a refiner's
3 fire, and like fuller's soap : And he shall sit *as* a refiner and purifier of silver : and he shall purify the sons of Levi, and purge them as gold and silver, that they may offer unto the
4 LORD an offering in righteousness. Then shall the offering of Judah and Jerusalem be pleasant unto the LORD, as in
5 the days of old, and as in former years. And I will come near to you to judgment ; and I will be a swift witness against the sorcerers, and against the adulterers, and against false swearers, and against those that oppress the hireling in *his* wages, the widow, and the fatherless, and that turn aside the stranger *from his right*, and fear not me, saith the LORD of hosts.

in the daily service. The Lord of the temple is further described as *the messenger* [angel] *of the covenant whom ye delight in*. No care is taken here or elsewhere to distinguish this angel of the covenant from Jehovah (see note on Zech. i. 11, and cp. Ex. iii. 2-6, xiv. 19, xxiii. 20, xxxiii. 14). The Jews *delighted in* Him, because they were under the impression that, by the mere fact of His coming, all their affairs would prosper. But, as ver. 2 reminds them, the facts were far otherwise.

2. The question with the people should have been, not, Will God never come? but, Are we prepared for His coming? *for He is like a refiner's fire, and like fuller's soap;* or, as His immediate herald said, "His fan is in His hand;" and again, "He shall baptize you with fire." No stain, no spurious goodness, could survive His coming; as fire burns out the slag and sifts it from the sound metal, as a chemical lye eats out impurities, so should the presence of the Messiah infallibly separate the true from the false, the seeming from the real, the bad from the good. [In the Anglo-Saxon gospels, John the Baptist is called *the fuller*.]

3. *And he shall sit as a refiner.* As if intent upon the work, and making no slight and passing business of it, He sits. Use may be made of the common observation that a refiner should go on with his work till he sees his own face reflected in the glowing metal. *He shall purify the sons of Levi.* "Judgment must begin at the house of God ;" they who were intended to represent in an especial way the holiness of God, and had charge of His house and worship, must first be cleansed, that the people may not be influenced for evil, but for good (see Neh. xiii. 30, and John ii. 13-22). Until the priests were clean, the offerings of the people could not be accepted (see ver. 14, and cp. Hag. ii. 10-14, with the notes). It was in the house of God He would meet with His people. But if that house itself was polluted, how could He approach them?

4. It need scarcely be said that this prediction gives no countenance to the idea that sacrifice continues in the Messianic times. Malachi speaks of the acceptable service of God's people in the terms of his own age.

5. The judgment, though it begins at the house of God, will extend to all the people. *I will be a swift witness against the sorcerers*, etc. Their challenge, Where is the God of judgment? will be answered. He will proceed against

6   For I *am* the LORD, I change not; therefore ye sons of
7   Jacob are not consumed. Even from the days of your fathers
ye are gone away from mine ordinances, and have not kept
them. Return unto me, and I will return unto you, saith the
LORD of hosts. But ye said, Wherein shall we return?
8   Will a man rob God? Yet ye have robbed me. But ye say,
Wherein have we robbed thee? In tithes and offerings.
9   Ye *are* cursed with a curse: for ye have robbed me, *even* this
10 whole nation. Bring ye all the tithes into the storehouse,
that there may be meat in mine house, and prove me now
herewith, saith the LORD of hosts, if I will not open you the
windows of heaven, and pour you out a blessing, that *there*

the actual sins which polluted the community. Lightfoot (xi. 208) says: "There was hardly any people in the whole world that more used or were more fond of amulets, charms, mutterings, exorcisms, and all kinds of enchantments." He also tells us (p. 301) that the elder who is chosen to sit in the Sanhedrim should be skilled in the arts of astrologers, jugglers, and sorcerers, that he may be able to judge those who are accused of practising such arts.

6, 7. *For I . . . are not consumed.* Ewald translates this verse: **For I, Jehovah, have not changed; but ye sons of Jacob, have ye not altered?** This meaning admirably fits the context. The delay complained of arises from no change in Jehovah, but from the decay of godliness in Israel. *Even from the days of your fathers ye are gone away from mine ordinances.* But in the face of the very similar language used in Ezra's prayer (Ezra ix. 14, 15), we must adhere to the meaning indicated in the English Version: **Because I, Jehovah, change not, therefore ye sons of Jacob are not consumed.** Already these sins mentioned in ver. 5 would have provoked the judgment of God, had not the purpose of the Eternal to make of Israel a delightsome land still held good. Even though generation after generation have departed from God, yet, **Return unto me, and I will return unto you, saith Jehovah of hosts.** The deep alienation between God and His people may yet be removed; and the Messiah they look for will come, if only they will even now repent. But so dull are they, they know not even that they have given offence or strayed: *Wherein*, they say, *shall we return?*

8. Their question admits of easy answer. They may *return* by rendering God His dues, by showing a regard to His service and upholding it with their means. They had robbed God by withholding tithes and offerings (see Neh. xiii. 10). The word *rob* might be better rendered **defraud**; and ver. 9 might be read, **Ye are cursed with the curse** [cp. ver. 11], **and yet ye go on defrauding me, even the whole nation.**

10. The *storehouse*, or, as Nehemiah calls it (xiii. 5), "a great chamber where they laid the meat-offerings, the frankincense, and the vessels, and the tithes of the corn, the new wine, and the oil." In response to this acknowledgment of Him, Jehovah will pour out a blessing upon them in those forms in which they seem mostly to need it, and to such an extent *that there shall not be room enough to receive it*, lit. **until a failure of sufficiency**, which Gesenius understands as meaning **until all my abundance be exhausted,**

11 *shall* not *be room* enough *to receive it.* And I will rebuke the devourer for your sakes, and he shall not destroy the fruits of your ground; neither shall your vine cast her fruit before the
12 time in the field, saith the LORD of hosts. And all nations shall call you blessed: for ye shall be a delightsome land, saith the LORD of hosts.
13 Your words have been stout against me, saith the LORD. Yet ye say, What have we spoken *so much* against thee?
14 Ye have said, It *is* vain to serve God: and what profit *is it* that we have kept his ordinance, and that we have walked
15 mournfully before the LORD of hosts? And now we call the proud happy; yea, they that work wickedness are set up; yea,
16 *they that* tempt God are even delivered. Then they that feared the LORD spake often one to another: and the LORD hearkened, and heard *it*, and a book of remembrance was written before him for them that feared the LORD, and that

that is, **for ever**, but which Ewald translates **until there is no more room** (cp. Zech. x. 10). The purport is plain: Subscribe liberally to charitable and religious objects even in bad times. It is your best investment.

11. *I will rebuke the devourer*, probably the **locust**. On the connection between liberality and prosperity, cp. Hag. i. 6-11, and the notes.

12. Cp. Isa. lxii. 4; Dan. xi. 16; Zech. vii. 14, viii. 13.

13-15. *Your words have been stout against me.* **Your words are insufferable,** they compel me to expostulate. The Hebrew conveys the idea of urgent insistance, or importunate iteration (cp. Ex. xii. 33). *Yet ye say, What have we spoken* so much *against thee*, or **conversed against thee?** It was in their talk with one another they had been instigated and drawn on to use the language referred to: **It is vain to serve God: and what profit is it that we have observed his observances, and that we have walked in mourning** [or gone in black, or gone dirty, as men fasting, not washing their faces nor anointing their heads]? God has said, All nations shall call us blessed; but it is **the proud we call blessed**: they are the men that are *set up*, that prosper in the world.

16. *Then*—that is, in consequence of the doubts uttered by the sceptical, and because of the need of mutual aid in maintaining faith—*they that feared the Lord spake often one to another*, **conversed one with another**, and conversed, of course, of this *fear of the Lord* which they cherished, and of the judgment they believed in. [Rabbi Chananiah ben Thradyon said: "Two that sit together and are occupied in words of Thorah have the Shekinah among them; for it is said, Then they that feared the Lord," etc. (*Pirke Aboth*, iii. 3). Cp. the Talmudic saying, "A great scholar profits from association with the meanest, as the small wood is used to set on fire the large: a disciple may be his master's best teacher" (Taylor's *Sayings of the Jewish Fathers*, p. 59).] For the important part played by this section of the community in those days, see Ezra ix. 4: "Then were assembled unto me every one that trembled at the words of the God of Israel," etc. *A book of remembrance was written.* An expression which is not borrowed from the practice of the

17 thought upon his name. And they shall be mine, saith the LORD of hosts, in that day when I make up my jewels; and I will spare them, as a man spareth his own son that serveth
18 him. Then shall ye return, and discern between the righteous and the wicked, between him that serveth God and him that serveth him not.

Persian monarchs alluded to in Esther vi. 1, but is a general anthropomorphism for observation and remembrance (cp. Isa. xxx. 8; Ex. xxxii. 32; Ps. lxix. 28, lvi. 8; Rev. iii. 5, xx. 12).

17. *And they . . . jewels;* better, **And they shall be to me a peculiar treasure, saith the Lord of hosts, in the day that I create [or prepare]**. The word rendered *jewels* is the word used in Ex. xix. 5, and there rendered *peculiar treasure;* its proper meaning is *private property*, and it is commonly used of Israel as the chosen portion of Jehovah. The words *in the day that I create*, are repeated in iv. 3, where this meaning is obvious (cp. Ps. cxviii. 24).

18. *Then shall ye return and discern*, rather, *And ye shall again discern*, as clearly as in the old days when God miraculously interposed to make a difference between His people and others.

CHAPTER IV.

1 FOR, behold, the day cometh, that shall burn as an oven; and all the proud, yea, and all that do wickedly, shall be stubble: and the day that cometh shall burn them up, saith the LORD of hosts, that it shall leave them neither root nor branch.
2 But unto you that fear my name shall the Sun of righteousness arise with healing in his wings; and ye shall go forth,
3 and grow up as calves of the stall. And ye shall tread down the wicked; for they shall be ashes under the soles of your feet in the day that I shall do *this*, saith the LORD of hosts.

1-3. A graphic presentation of these verses is given by Stanley (*Jewish Ch.* iii. 158). The day spoken of "was to be like the glorious but terrible uprising of the eastern sun which should wither to the very roots the insolence and the injustice of mankind, but, as its rays extended, like the wings of the Egyptian sun-god, should by its healing and invigorating influences call forth the good from their obscurity, prancing and bounding like the young cattle in the burst of spring, and treading down under their feet the dust and ashes to which the same bright sun had burnt up the tangled thicket of iniquitous dealing." *All the proud, yea, and all that do wickedly, i.e.* all those who seemed for the present to be prospering in spite of God (cp. iii. 15), as the designation *you that fear my name* comprises those who, in spite of present appearances, still believed that God hates wickedness (cp. iii. 16). "Light is sown for the upright;" unto such *the Sun of righteousness shall arise with*

4 Remember ye the law of Moses my servant, which I commanded unto him in Horeb for all Israel, *with* the statutes
5 and judgments. Behold, I will send you Elijah the prophet before the coming of the great and dreadful day of the LORD:
6 And he shall turn the heart of the fathers to the children, and the heart of the children to their fathers, lest I come and smite the earth with a curse.

healing in his wings, or, **in his beams**. God's righteous judgment shall shed light upon all the perplexed and dark ways of men: this is the consolation and hope afforded by the prophet to those who felt it difficult to maintain faith in a sceptical backsliding age. "Fret not thyself because of evil-doers. Commit thy way unto the Lord. Trust in Him. And He shall bring forth thy righteousness as the light, and thy judgment as the noonday." It is the counterpart of the constant appeal in the Psalms to God's *righteousness*. It is a promise which survives in the N. T. in the form, "God is not unrighteous to forget your work." They that fear the Lord with believing reverence wait for the manifestation of His righteousness, conscious that they love God, that they seek first His kingdom and His righteousness. They shall thrive in that air and element; they *shall go forth, and grow up as calves of the stall*, or **leap as stall-fed calves**, which when let out to the fields caper and frolic in the exuberance of healthy life.

4. *Remember ye the law.* Do not be carried away by new views of duty and of your relation to God. Do not suffer yourselves to be perplexed by apparent irregularities in His government, by the prosperity of the wicked and the misery of the righteous. Adhere to the plain way of duty. "The secret things belong to the Lord;" be it yours to obey His commands. Cp. the strikingly similar conclusion to the book of Ecclesiastes: "Let us hear the conclusion of the whole matter: Fear God and keep His commandments." Cp. also the reponement of the law by Ezra in the mind and life of Israel.

5, 6. *Behold, I will send you Elijah . . . curse.* A prophet would be sent to prepare the people, that when that burning day came they might be of a quality incombustible. That the coming of the Lord might not *smite the earth with a curse* (cp. note on Zech. xiv. 11, and an admirable note in Maclear's *Joshua*, p. 59), preparation must be made by hearty penitence and zealous return to the law. *The heart of the fathers must be turned to the children, and the heart of the children to the fathers.* The new era must be prepared for by a return to the old, and that which was the essence of the old must not grudge to develope into new forms and attain its designed end and fruit. Not by getting rid of the law, but by fulfilling it, is preparation made for what is higher than the law, for the grace and reality that come by Jesus Christ. Not by turning the back upon Moses and the fathers generally will the children attain to their golden future; but not by shutting up their children under the iron bars of the law will the fathers reach the promises which they themselves believed in, but by trusting their children to move on and play their part also in the development of God's plan. (The passage which seems to throw most light on the phraseology of ver. 6 is Isa. xxix. 22–24, cp. Luke i. 17.) Why is *Elijah* the designation given to this prophet, and why is it *he* who appears at the Transfiguration along with Moses? He is chosen as the representative of the prophetic order, because for courage, force, and personal influence in his generation no prophet surpassed or equalled him. He, more than any other, was "a voice;" God's message to the people, detached from earthly pursuits and living as if sent out from God's presence to do His bidding for a little and return. So came John the Baptist (cp. Matt. xi. 14, xvii. 12), although himself denying that he was Elias (John i. 21), because of the superstitious belief that had grown up to the effect that Elijah was kept in hiding and would in his own person return as the Messiah's herald.

REMARKS.—1. It is quite fair reasoning when the human heart, conscious of its integrity, claims to profit by its integrity; it is the instinctive acknowledgment that we are under a moral government. But it is a mistake to insist that circumstances should at once and in every instance correspond with conduct and character. If it were so, this would be no training school for men. If the righteous were immediately rewarded, if every transgression of the moral law were as quickly followed by pain as every transgression of physical law is, then virtue and pleasure would be so confounded that we could never know whether it was the one or the other of things so essentially different that we were choosing.

2. We are situated now between two days of the Lord. The day which the Lord hath made has shone upon us (Luke i. 78), yet the Sun of Righteousness is to shine out again still more powerfully. It is in a manner *set* for the present. We are as in an arctic night, the after-glow of sunset enduring and merging only in the dawn of the new day. Or we live in a brilliant moonlight, the reflected light giving us evidence of the continued existence of our Sun.

> *Draw out from the materials furnished by the books of Ezra and Nehemiah a picture of the social state pointed at in iii. 5.*
>
> *What were the tithes required by the law? What recent enactment rendered their non-payment in Malachi's time specially heinous?*
>
> *Compare Malachi's representation of the day of the Lord with that given by the other prophets.*
>
> The Sun of Righteousness. *Does this mean the light which is brought when the righteous judgment of God appears,* i.e. *the Sun which is righteousness? or does it mean the Sun which produces righteousness? Explain fully how Christ is such a Sun, and how He sifted good men from bad.*
>
> *What practical benefit results from the present impunity of wicked men and the delayed reward of the righteous? And what is the best reward of the righteous?*
>
> *In iii. 7 Israel is called God's* peculium; *show the connection between early wealth and large flocks and herds, as illustrated by the words* pecunia, cattle *and* chattels, heads *of* cattle *and* capital, fee *and German* Vieh, cattle.
>
> *Learn the hymn, " Christ whose glory fills the skies."*

www.ingramcontent.com/pod-product-compliance
Lightning Source LLC
Chambersburg PA
CBHW022125160426
43197CB00009B/1160